yourseiᴛ

intellectual property

in association with **The Telegraph BUSINESSCLUB**

intellectual property
miles rees and
lawrence smith-higgins

For over 60 years, more than
50 million people have learnt over
750 subjects the **teach yourself**
way, with impressive results.

be where you want to be
with **teach yourself**

in association with **The Telegraph BUSINESSCLUB**

For UK order enquiries: please contact Bookpoint Ltd, 130 Milton Park, Abingdon, Oxon, OX14 4SB. Telephone: +44 (0) 1235 827720. Fax: +44 (0) 1235 400454. Lines are open 09.00–17.00, Monday to Saturday, with a 24-hour message answering service. Details about our titles and how to order are available at www.teachyourself.co.uk

Long renowned as the authoritative source for self-guided learning – with more than 50 million copies sold worldwide – the **teach yourself** series includes over 500 titles in the fields of languages, crafts, hobbies, business, computing and education.

British Library Cataloguing in Publication Data: a catalogue record for this title is available from the British Library.

ISBN-10: 0340 926732
ISBN-13: 978 0340 926734

First published in UK 2006 by Hodder Education, 338 Euston Road, London, NW1 3BH.

This edition published 2006.

The **teach yourself** name is a registered trade mark of Hodder Headline.

Copyright © 2006 Miles Rees and Lawrence Smith-Higgins, and Ron Hamilton for section 2.2

Typeset by Transet Limited, Coventry, England.
Printed in Great Britain for Hodder Education, a division of Hodder Headline, 338 Euston Road, London, NW1 3BH, by Cox & Wyman Ltd, Reading, Berkshire.

The publisher has used its best endeavours to ensure that the URLs for external websites referred to in this book are correct and active at the time of going to press. However, the publisher and the author have no responsibility for the websites and can make no guarantee that a site will remain live or that the content will remain relevant, decent or appropriate.

Hodder Headline's policy is to use papers that are natural, renewable and recyclable products and made from wood grown in sustainable forests. The logging and manufacturing processes are expected to conform to the environmental regulations of the country of origin.

Impression number   10 9 8 7 6 5 4 3 2 1
Year   2010 2009 2008 2007 2006

contents

	contributors	**ix**
	introduction	**1**
	Why intellectual property is important, why it matters	1
	Lord Sainsbury of Turville	
01	**intellectual property rights**	**7**
	1.1 What is intellectual property?	8
	Miles Rees	
	1.2 The essentials of patenting	10
	Gwilym Roberts	
	1.3 The essentials of trade marks	14
	Richard Gallafent	
	1.4 The essentials of design registration	19
	Gary Townley	
	1.5 The essentials of copyright	23
	Jill Durdin	
	1.6 The essentials of domain name registration	26
	Miles Rees	
02	**intellectual property and the business perspective**	**29**
	2.1 Business adviser networks	30
	Iain Russell	
	2.2 Making money from intellectual property	33
	Ron Hamilton	
03	**building your intellectual property**	**39**
	3.1 The intellectual property audit	40
	Lawrence Smith-Higgins	
	3.2 Searching intellectual property databases	49
	Jeremy Philpott	
	3.3 Licensing your intellectual property	58
	Christi Mitchell	

04	**working with universities**	**69**
4.1	Collaborative research and development *Lawrence Cullen*	70
4.2	Making money from intellectual property *Dave Morgan*	77
05	**Looking after your intellectual property**	**81**
5.1	Looking after your patent *Gwilym Roberts*	82
5.2	Looking after your trade marks *Tom Farrand*	86
5.3	Looking after your designs *Chris Lewis*	90
5.4	Looking after your copyright *Jill Durdin*	94
5.5	Intellectual property insurance *Margaret Briffa*	98
5.6	Enforcement of intellectual property rights *Phil Lewis*	104
5.7	Companies and the law *Brenda Hannigan*	111
06	**around the world**	**118**
6.1	European patent protection *Jeremy Philpott*	119
6.2	International patent protection: strategic issues for SMEs *Esteban Burrone*	125
6.3	European trade mark protection *Peter Lawrence*	132
6.4	International trade mark protection: why and how? *Esteban Burrone*	137
6.5	The Community design *Peter Lawrence*	143
6.6	International copyright protection *Jill Durdin*	148

07 **help from others** **149**

7.1 National Endowment for Science, Technology
and the Arts 150
Eddie Tuttle

7.2 Inventor clubs 154
Linda Oakley

7.3 Step-by-step guide to using invention promoters 157
Miles Rees

7.4 Manufacturing Advisory Service 161
Colin Allaway

7.5 DTI business support solutions 165
Miles Rees

7.6 The Design Council 169
Jan Dekker

taking it further **172**
index **175**

contributors

This book wouldn't have been possible without the help and cooperation of its contributors. They all have expertise of Intellectual Property through providing professional advice or running their own business. Their help/contribution is gratefully acknowledged and they are listed below.

Colin Allaway, Principal Manufacturing Specialist, The Manufacturing Advisory Service (MAS) (section 7.4)

Margaret Briffa, Intellectual Property Lawyer, Briffa, London (section 5.5)

Esteban Burrone, Consultant, SMEs Division, World Intellectual Property Organization (WIPO), Geneva (sections 6.2 and 6.4)

Lawrence Cullen, Secretariat to the Lambert Working Group on Intellectual Property, The Patent Office (section 4.1)

Jan Dekker, The Design Council (section 7.6)

Jill Durdin, Marketing Executive, The Patent Office (sections 1.5, 5.4 and 6.6)

Tom Farrand, Trade Mark Attorney, ip21, London (section 5.2)

Richard Gallafent, Patent and Trade Mark Attorney, Gallafent & Co (section 1.3)

Ron Hamilton, Chairman, Daysoft® Limited (section 2.2)

Brenda Hannigan, Professor of Corporate Law, University of Southampton (section 5.7)

Peter Lawrence, Vice-President, Office of Harmonization for the Internal Market (OHIM) (sections 6.3 and 6.5)

Chris Lewis, Business Events Manager, The Patent Office (section 5.3)

Phil Lewis, Senior Policy Adviser, The Patent Office (section 5.6)

Christi Mitchell, IP Director, Highbury Ltd (section 3.3)

Dave Morgan, Education and Enterprise Manager, The Patent Office (section 4.2)

Linda Oakley, ideas 21 (section 7.2)

Jeremy Philpott, Innovation Support Unit Manager, European Patent Academy (sections 3.2 and 6.1)

Miles Rees, Business Development Manager, The Patent Office (sections 1.1, 1.6, 7.3 and 7.5)

Gwilym Roberts, Patent Attorney, Kilburn & Strode, London (sections 1.2 and 5.1)

Iain Russell, Chief Executive, Intellectual Assets Centre (section 2.1)

Lord Sainsbury of Turville (Introduction)

Lawrence Smith-Higgins, Head of Awareness, Information and Media, The Patent Office (section 3.1)

Gary Townley, Business Events Manager, The Patent Office (section 1.4)

Eddie Tuttle, Senior Policy Adviser, National Endowment for Science, Technology and the Arts (NESTA) (section 7.1)

Why intellectual property is important, why it matters . . .

You are all no doubt aware of the immense changes in the global economy, as Asia moves towards the centre stage. As barriers to world trade come down, we have to compete head-to-head with countries like China where wage costs are just 5 per cent of ours. Like our competitors, we have witnessed a significant shift in our economy from traditional manufacturing towards knowledge economies based on creativity and innovation. In this new world, modifying our focus is central to our economic success.

And we are doing so. We lead Europe in knowledge-based and high-tech businesses such as aerospace and pharmaceuticals. Knowledge-based business services have accounted for over half of our job growth in the past two decades. And we have a very strong position in the creative industries.

These kinds of industries place even more emphasis on the value of intellectual property (IP). IP underpins their businesses, allowing them to make a return on their investment, even in the initial stages, helping them gain access to finance.

IP debate

The allocation of IP is both democratic and fair. Rights are not based on the size of the company or the popularity of an individual but on the quality of the invention or in the case of copyright, the creative input without prejudice to the perceived quality. So IP rewards inventors in their garages or the composer in his or her bedroom as much as a big pharmaceutical company or a pop superstar. They are awarded the same rights and the same conditions and privileges.

Perhaps this is why IP has moved from being considered an obscure branch of law, to becoming the focus of intense debate amongst users and consumers.

Much of this debate focuses wrongly, I believe, either on the relative merits of one type of IP over another, or sets 'IP' against 'free access'.

But this misunderstands the current situation as it assumes a regime in which Government not only upholds the rights but dictates how they should be exploited.

The true strength of the UK's IP system lies in the flexibility it provides to creators to exploit their ideas and their creativity as they see fit. And EMI is a prime example: today we see it as a copyright-based company. But its founder was the inventor of the gramophone, and its patents cover radar and CAT scanners. Like many of our global leaders, EMI has successfully used a variety of IP rights.

But if a flexible system is to be an asset, it must also be robust – that robustness should come not only from a system able to cope with the development of innovative new technologies, but also able to promote innovation in the widest sense. And it will fail to do that if it becomes too prescriptive.

So what is Government's role? Government must ensure a proper balance between the benefits and incentives for the consumer and the creator. It must recognize that different sectors have distinctive business models. It must recognise that almost every industry uses a mix of the different forms of IP. So the rights must be able to work alongside each other in a complementary but distinctive way, to give industry the flexibility to choose.

Above all, Government must resist calls to dictate to creators how they should exploit their rights.

Copyright

Copyright gives creators the confidence to share and disseminate their work, safe in the knowledge that they are protected should someone try to copy or steal their work without consent. How creators choose to share their IP is up to them, but IP provides options for them to exploit their work to their own advantage.

The Artic Monkeys and Sandi Thom provide novel examples of the use of IP – effectively 'giving away' their music via the Internet to create customer demand and grab the attention of record companies. They could only do this because of the flexibility and robustness within the copyright system, and because the digital age offers new business models to anyone with the will to exploit their works: home computing allows for production studios at home and distribution via the Internet. But ultimately, many creators will want the backing of copyright to give them some sort of protection, whether they seek appropriate payment, or recognition from someone wanting to use their work.

Of course copyright seeks to reward creativity, not to stifle it. Exclusive rights are granted to the creator for a limited period of time, but there is heated debate about the length of that period. It should be fair, proportionate and based on economic evidence. It should not disadvantage our creators and creative industries, but equally should not unreasonably prevent others from building on creativity by re-using and adding value to works that become available. A difficult balance – but important that we get it right.

Patents

Whilst copyright provides protection for some aspects of creativity – such as music, films and games software – patents provide important protection for industrial and scientific creativity. Like all IP, patents are optional: some may choose not to use them, but for research-intensive industries they provide a valuable means of protecting their investment. And, like all IP, they don't come with instructions for use. It's up to the rights owner to decide how to exploit their patent. That might be by licensing others to produce the invention, by encouraging collaboration, as Microsoft is doing with its 'IP Venture Licensing Programme',[1] by producing products themselves, or, as IBM has done with some software patents, making them freely available.

---

[1] www.microsoft.com/mscorp/ip/ventures

It is important to ensure that the patent system only supports genuine innovation: inappropriate patents are not helpful to owners, users or competitors. That is why the Patent Office – in its role as administrator – is currently considering responses to a consultation on whether the level of inventive step in the UK is appropriate. We don't want patents to become defensive tools preventing innovation.

Enforcement

Having flexibility also means having responsibility as a society to respect and value the creations of others, backed up by a rigorous enforcement strategy.

Enforcement has become an increasingly challenging area as we continue to fight the importation of fake goods but equally challenging is the rise of the digital environment. Its impact on both production and distribution of fakes is a new challenge for us. Fake CDs and DVDs no longer need to be produced elsewhere and smuggled into the country as new technology means they can be produced in a small flat anywhere in the UK. Digitization also means that illegal distribution and theft can occur computer to computer without a physical copy ever being produced.

Unfortunately we are not the only ones to have recognized the increased value of IP in today's world. Historically, crime has always followed the economy and as the knowledge-based economy provides more opportunities, that is where criminal elements have moved.

Let's be clear. IP crime is not a victimless crime: fake goods often compromise health and safety, or lure innocent purchasers in to committing criminal acts, as seen recently with the Russian MP3 website. Neither is IP crime limited to one-man bands: we have evidence that people involved in IP theft are organized criminals. Proceeds from IP crime fund other types of crime, such as drugs and organized crime. We want a safe environment for business and our communities to grow and develop. We don't want IP crime to harm society either in lost jobs or poor-quality products. We're determined to stamp this out. That's why we have a National IP Crime Strategy.

Led by the Patent Office it brings together a range of partners to tackle IP theft strategically. It has led to the development of TellPat, a national database for recording counterfeiting and piracy activities, and to a series of raids at Wembley market at the end of 2005 which netted more than 1.5 million pounds-worth of counterfeit goods. As a result approximately 34 people are being prosecuted, with intelligence also passed to other agencies for action.

So the message to the criminals is that the UK is no longer a safe environment for you. Our joint intelligence will lead to more surprise raids, in more locations, and we will take action against all those who are involved.

And we do not intend to let IP criminals flourish elsewhere. We recognize that this is not just a UK problem. So internationally, we are helping our partners to deal with problems in their own countries. In China, for example, the Patent Office has been training police in the use of intelligence, and promoting best practice – developed in the UK – to prevent and disrupt IP crime.

Flexibility

The flexibility needed within the system applies to those with responsibility for the system too. For the Patent Office this includes looking not only at enforcement and administrative issues, but at awareness raising too. Businesses, would-be inventors, consumers – in particular the young – need to be aware of IP, its role and their responsibilities. Programmes such as THINK Kit, 'What is the Key?' and the Lambert Model Agreements all help. And these issues – administration, awareness and enforcement – form three of the strands for the Patent Office's new business model: 'A Patent Office for the 21st Century'.

The flexibilities in the system are a good thing, but should not be confused with uncertainty about what can be protected. Businesses and consumers need to be sure about what they can and cannot lawfully do. Consumer confusion over the copying of their own CDs onto their MP3 players is not helpful. And advances in technology need not always be seen as threats. The economy has always benefited from new technologies – look at trains, computers and videos – that were initially seen as a threat to the old world order.

Conclusion

I hope I have demonstrated that, rather than arguing 'all or nothing', we need a more sophisticated debate about IP, which recognizes the complexity of the system. It is not Government's job to dictate to creators how to exploit the protection they have, but to ensure that they have the opportunity to do so in a way that helps and encourages them to be innovative. So let's have a real conversation about how we ensure that the UK – with our strengths in ideas and creativity – has a robust IP system which allows us to flourish in the global knowledge economy.

In the new global economy innovation has a central role to play in economic success, and we need to make certain that we have a system of intellectual property rights which is fit for the twenty-first century.

Lord Sainsbury of Turville

01

intellectual property rights

In this chapter you will learn:

- the importance of IP to business
- what can be patented
- how you protect a trade mark and design
- about copyright protection
- about registering domain names

1.1 What is intellectual property

The importance of intellectual property to businesses

Every product or service that we use in our daily lives is the result of a long chain of big or small innovations, such as changes in design or improvements that make a product look or function the way it does today. Take for example the mobile telephone, the technology can be traced back to an idea pioneered by the Hollywood actress Hedy Lamarr back in the 1940s which was seen as a breakthrough in the area of communication. Many others have since improved the design and function of such products, and legally protected their improvements through the acquisition of IP rights.

This is likely to be the case with almost any product or service in the marketplace. Everything from a tube of toothpaste to the latest MP3 player will have Intellectual Property which can be protected. The chemical formula or technical parts can be protected by patents, the shape or appearance can be protected by registered design, the brand name can be protected by trade marks and any artwork or music is protected by copyright.

How does this affect your business?

Regardless of what product your business makes or what service it provides, it is likely that you are using and creating intellectual property. Almost every business will have a trade name or a trade mark and should consider protecting them. Many will have valuable confidential business information that they may wish to protect. Others may have developed creative original designs or invented a new process.

Why should you use IP?

Intellectual property may assist you in almost every aspect of your business development and competitive strategy, from product development to marketing. It may also be an important factor when considering exporting or expanding your business abroad.

Trade marks are in many ways the face of your business; they allow your customers to distinguish your products and services from your competitors. They are also seen as a guarantee of consistent quality; a customer who is pleased with your product or service will continue to purchase it based on the quality expectations of the known trade mark.

Registered design adds value to a product by creating variety in a world of commodities. Aesthetically pleasing design helps build trust and lasting customer relationships which translate into higher market share, better prices and bigger profits.

Patent protection, if your company has invested a significant amount of time and money in research and design, could help in recovering costs and obtaining higher returns on investments. A patent owner may also license their rights in exchange for royalties to generate additional income.

Copyright in some form is owned by most businesses. Although they may not be directly involved in making money from their copyright, businesses print brochures, publish advertisements and own websites that contain copyright-protected materials.

The creation and development of new technologies and industries, and the encouragement of growth of commerce, is essential to the economic well-being of the United Kingdom. To achieve advances in these areas depends not only on the ingenuity of scientists, engineers, and others, but also on the investment necessary to develop new ideas and set up new enterprises as well as the ability to market them effectively.

Intellectual property rights play an important role in bringing these various factors together.

In all cases, they give legal recognition to the ownership of new ideas or new brands and give the proprietors the right to stop other people exploiting their property.

The Patent Office is responsible for granting patents, registered designs, and registered trade marks. Since all these rights are essentially territorial, the UK Patent Office grants rights that are effective in the UK only. International protection is dealt with later, but it should be noted that the European Patent Convention and the Patent Cooperation Treaty also provide methods of obtaining patent protection in the UK.

More information on all forms of intellectual property and the role the Patent Office plays in protecting it can be found at www.patent.gov.uk or tel: 08459 500 505.

1.2 The essentials of patenting

What can be patented?

When they first appeared, several hundred years ago, patents were handed out as favours and could confer monopolies for any kind of subject matter. In time this was seen as being unfair on the public at large and it was decided that patents should only be given for inventions. The immediate problem, therefore, was to decide what an invention was and this has been the subject of much legal debate for many years. Nowadays a reasonably objective test has been developed to determine whether something is a 'patentable invention' although the legal debate continues on a case-by-case basis as to whether a particular concept meets the requirement or not.

Fundamentally, patents relate to technical concepts, and in particular the underlying features that make them advantageous. In order to assess patentability, a new concept described in a patent is tested against everything in the public domain before the patent was first filed (in the US, in some cases an extra one-year 'grace period' is sometimes available). This public domain information is usually termed the 'prior art'. The test is in fact twofold, with the two limbs being novelty and inventive step.

The first question, therefore, is 'is the subject matter novel?'. In order to have novelty it must be different from the prior art. However, as far as novelty is concerned, just *how* different does not matter.

In order, then, to ensure that patents were not granted for trivially different concepts the second test of 'inventive step' (sometimes termed 'non-obviousness') is also applied. Having identified the difference between the new concept and prior art, the next question therefore is 'is it inventively different?'. To introduce objectivity the test is applied from the point of view of the 'nominally skilled person' who is someone considered to understand the technical field but to have no inventive capacity themselves. One of the most simple and effective tests for inventiveness is the 'problem–solution' test which has been developed by the European Patent Office. According to that test, once you have identified the novel difference over the prior art you then identify whether it solves a technical problem with the prior art. If so, then you have a patentable invention.

Patentability is also limited in most jurisdictions to certain types of subject matter. For example, in Europe the patent must relate to technical subject matter rather than, for example, mathematical methods, business methods or discoveries. An area of particular interest has been that of patenting computer programs. Many people have heard that it is not possible to patent computer programs in Europe but the reality is rather different from this. In fact thousands of patents are granted every year in Europe relating to computer programs and the actual test is whether the computer program has a technical effect. Often, for example, computer programs are used to implement business methods such as financial trading systems. If the computer program is merely automating a trading system that was previously done manually then it is not considered to involve a technical effect. If, however, the computer is used cleverly such that its operation or data storage is enhanced in conjunction with implementation of the trading system then a technical effect may be there and a patent may be available.

Similarly issues have arisen, at least in Europe, in relation to the medical and pharmaceutical areas. For example, methods of surgery, treatment or diagnosis are not patentable although the corresponding apparatus (for example an X-ray machine) is, the idea being that the patent system should not stop doctors saving people's lives. In the world of biotechnology there are also exclusions for example to deal with ethical concerns. For example, genes can be patented but only if the function of the gene is known.

What does a patent look like?

The structure of a patent is specifically designed to ensure that it meets the requirement of providing a monopoly that does not impinge unfairly on third parties. It can effectively be split in two parts, a 'description' and 'claims'.

The description serves various functions. First of all it sets out the prior art which the patentee is aware of and outlines problems with the prior art that the invention addresses. The most important part of the description then follows in the form of a description of a 'specific embodiment' of the invention. This is the part where the invention is described in enough detail that the skilled reader could put the invention into effect – the 'sufficiency' requirement. Typically, one or more examples of a detailed implementation of the invention are described. This does not necessarily limit the protection afforded by the patent – the invention may be a fairly broad concept that can be implemented in various ways some of which may not even have been worked out by the inventor yet. It is always worthwhile putting a lot of effort into the description to stop third parties from challenging the patent, asserting that it does not describe the invention sufficiently. This is especially the case as it is not possible to add information to the document later in its life (barring a slight amount of latitude in the first year) – hence it is always best to err on the side of describing too much rather than too little.

The part of the patent which is usually most alien to the layperson is the claims. These comprise clauses at the end of the patent document which define what third parties cannot do without infringing the patent. In particular the claims define the concept in the context of core technical features which any implementation of the invention would share. The claims take the form typically of method claims defining a set of technical steps involved in the invention and apparatus claims defining the physical features. Of course they are written to cover as much as possible. However, they cannot go too far because then they will start covering the prior art, or non-inventive modifications of the prior art, and hence will be unpatentable. Well-drafted claims also include multiple fall-back positions in order to deal with eventualities such as third parties or patent offices challenging the claims on the basis of prior art the patentees had not been aware of, bearing in mind, once again, that it is not permissible to add to the information content of a patent application once it has been filed.

Getting a patent

So far the discussion has been directed to patents but in fact the first stage in the life of a patent is the application stage. This starts with the filing of an application for a patent before a patent office, which will then carry out a search to see whether there is relevant prior art preceding the filing date of the application. The application is published 18 months from its earliest date and the patent application is then examined, principally to ensure that it meets the novelty and inventive step criteria based on the searched prior art, but also to check issues such as sufficiency and clarity. If the examination is unfavourable then the patentee has one or more opportunities to respond with either argumentation or modification of the patent application –

termed an 'amendment' – within the constraints of not adding new information. Once the examination is favourable then the patent can proceed to grant.

During the application phase the patent application provides a restricted degree of 'provisional protection' and only after it is granted can it be enforced against third parties, for example by suing them. However, licences can be awarded throughout. The patent application can remain pending for several years but generally users of the system are happy with this because of the provisional protection it affords and because it delays the general expense of the procedure

Generally speaking patents are granted country by country and hence Patent Office by Patent Office. There are some regional systems in place which reduce duplication, however. The European Patent Office for example is able to grant patents across a territory which includes the EU and various other territories.

There are various strategies to obtain a patent in multiple countries but one of the major considerations is the cost of the procedure which is more or less proportional to the number of countries. A typical strategy is to make use of the 'priority' system, allowing the patentee to file an initial patent application in a single country and, within one year of that initial filing, to file overseas applications. At the end of the one year, a particularly cost effective way of keeping the patent application pending for as many territories as possible is to file an international patent application (sometimes known as a Patent Cooperation Treaty (PCT) application). This effectively keeps the patent pending for a further 18 months but, importantly, does not result in an international patent. At the end of the additional 18 months the patentee must then transfer to the patent application to each of the specific territories of interest and after that it is dealt with as a normal patent application in each of those countries, but as though it had been filed at the same time as the initial application. As a result the patentee effectively has two and a half years from the initial filing to make a final decision on what countries to obtain protection in.

Whichever overseas filing strategy is adopted, once the patent has been examined and any objections overcome it is granted territory by territory. The length of time it takes and the changes needed may vary between countries such that the patent protection is not identical, although it is fairly unusual for the protection to differ radically between jurisdictions.

Once the patent has been granted it is necessary to keep it alive – 'in force' – by payment of renewal fees, sometimes termed annuities. Typically such fees are required every year although in the US they are spaced out rather more. The patent dies if the renewal fee is not paid or after 20 years from the date it was filed. In certain areas of technology the life can be extended further using 'Supplementary Protection Certificates'. For example, in the case of pharmaceuticals, where regulatory processes delay marketing of a drug, some of this lost time can be regained.

Using the patent

The main purpose of the patent is to serve as an exclusive right giving the patentee the opportunity of preventing third parties from using the invention. In its most radical form, therefore, the patentee can sue an infringer and, if successful, obtain an injunction against further infringement as well as damages for lost sales and so forth. Often of course this option is used as a bargaining tool to obtain a favourable agreement between parties where the patentee will be satisfied with a licensing royalty.

Another effective use of the patent is as part of a patent licensing strategy, bearing in mind that patents can be licensed with more than one party and the licensing schemes can vary between territories.

A further use of patents which is becoming more prevalent is their use in raising funding for early-stage companies. Such companies may not yet have any products and so can only be valued based on their intellectual property and a strong and well-drafted patent portfolio can be extremely important in attracting investment.

1.3 The essentials of trade marks

The nature of a trade mark

Throughout the world, products and services are promoted under names or symbols which distinguish one product or service from another of the same type. Advertising uses such names or symbols to promote repeat business, and, in the case of consumer goods, selection of the advertised product from a range of similar ones on the supermarket shelf. Distinction is usually conferred by using as an identifier something which does not directly refer (though it may allude) to the nature of the goods or service in question, for example Apple for computers, eBay for internet sales.

Other types of identifier are sometimes used, for example a sound such as a jingle, a colour, a particular shape or a smell, but these are unusual and sometimes rather difficult to operate in practice, as they are often not seen by the user or consumer as performing the same identification function.

The name, symbol or other distinctive identifier chosen is called a trade mark (often written as one word in the USA).

Most trade marks identify origin, indicating that the goods or services come from a particular source (or that the product or service is provided under the authority of a single trade mark owner – as in a franchise operation). Trade marks which have other functions do exist, for example certification or guarantee marks, which means that certain standards are met, or collective marks, which can be used by any member of the organization which owns them.

Signs which are merely descriptive of the product or service do not function as trade marks: for example Apple is no good as a trade mark for apples as it simply says what they are. Nor are words which describe a characteristic of the goods or services or which are commonly used in connection with the provision of either, for example laudatory words such as 'super' or 'ultra-effective'. A picture of the goods is likewise not distinctive.

In contrast, a purely invented word or new fanciful design is inherently distinctive, and for any goods or services. In the case of known words, distinctiveness depends on context: 'Megabyte' is descriptive for computer memory devices, but would be distinctive as the name of a pop group or in respect of articles of clothing.

Between the extremes of distinctiveness and descriptiveness come marks which are not particularly distinctive to start with, but which, usually following promotion and a lot of actual use, become distinctive. For example, the title *Business Week*, when first launched, was simply descriptive of the content and frequency of publication. After decades of use, and with no one else using it as well, the title becomes distinctive and can be registered as a trade mark.

The reverse process can occur: a mark which starts out as distinctive can become generic (and thus cease to act as a trade mark) if care is not taken to use the mark always as an adjective – never as a verb or noun, e.g. not a 'Hoover', but a 'Hoover vacuum cleaner', and to suppress any use of the mark by others.

Protecting trade marks

Trade marks may be protected by registering at a Trade Mark Office. That Office maintains an official register of marks, giving the details of the mark, the goods and the owner. The purpose of this open public register is to provide third parties with notice of your claim, so that they can see who has the rights in any particular sign.

The main such right is the right to stop other people using the same or a similar mark in a way which leads to, or could lead to, confusion.

To register you must precisely identify the mark the goods or services in respect of which you want registration, and apply to register formally at the Trade Marks Office. The Office will then decide whether the mark applied for is something which can, in respect of the goods or services specified, act as a distinctive identifier.

The Office may also carry out a search among marks already registered with it to see if anyone else has already registered (or applied to register) a similar mark for similar goods or services. If they have, you may have to overcome an objection from the Trade Mark Office (or from the earlier mark owner) if registration is to be achieved. Earlier owners have a chance to object during an 'opposition period' which starts when the Trade Mark Office publishes the details of the mark. If an earlier right holder, for example a user of a similar mark, objects, the Office will resolve the opposition one way or the other. This can take some time.

You can apply to register before the mark is used; this can enable protection to be obtained before a new product or service is launched.

Once you have your registration, you may legitimately adopt wording or the ® symbol used in conjunction with the mark to indicate that it is registered (before this occurs, people often use the superscript ™ to indicate that the word or sign it accompanies is regarded as a trade mark by its owner).

Thereafter, if anyone else, 'the infringer', uses the same or a similar mark on the same or similar goods or services, you can take action to prevent such activity continuing. If, following a polite request to stop, the infringer refuses, then serious consideration must be given to taking action through the courts. You have to police your registration – the Trade Mark Office will not do it for you.

It is a common misconception that registration of your name, either by way of the registration of a company or by way of registration of an Internet domain, provides some form of protection. Essentially it does not. Company registration offices and Internet domain name registrars are essentially concerned merely to avoid confusion by ensuring that no two persons have exactly the same name.

International aspects

Most countries have their own Trade Mark Office. In addition, there is a Community Trade Mark Office which provides registration with effect throughout the European Union.

Over 70 countries are also members of an arrangement (called 'Madrid' for short) providing for the so-called 'international' registration of a trade mark. A trade mark owner who has a 'home' registration, usually in that owner's home country, may apply on the basis of it for an international registration.

When applying for an international registration, you have to indicate what countries you wish the international registration to cover; the cost depends on how many are chosen. The EU can be chosen as a single 'designation'.

Under the international system, the Trade Mark Office which operates the system (the Madrid International Bureau of the World Intellectual Property Organisation, Geneva) grants essentially a bundle of national registrations, each to be considered as 'provisional'. Local objections can arise in any specific designation and, if they do, the owner can choose to contest the objections or to let that designation lapse.

In countries where there is no objection, then the international registration is fully effective and provides the same rights as a registration obtained direct from its national Trade Mark Office.

After international registration has been achieved, further countries can be added later to expand the geographical protection.

Assignment and licensing

A trade mark registration may be sold and purchased, i.e. the rights can shift from one party to another. This often happens when established businesses acquire or divest themselves of particular brands.

The rights which are given by registration may be licensed to third parties, i.e. the mark owner can, if desired, let other people use the mark. This is of particular value in connection with the provision of services where the core identity of a franchised business is the (usually very heavily protected) trade mark in question.

Limitations of registration

The rights given by a registration are not absolute, i.e. they do not prevent anyone else without permission using the sign in question, though care should be taken whenever people use someone else's mark. For example, the use of a mark in a newspaper report is entirely legitimate, as may be used, for example, by an auto repair engineer to indicate the brand or models of vehicle in which he or she is an expert.

Non-use

If a mark is not used, or if it is used, but the use is discontinued, after a certain time, the registration becomes vulnerable to removal from the register, at the request of a third party.

Trade mark clearance

Because there are hundreds of thousands of marks registered in respect of a huge variety of goods and services, anyone contemplating setting up a business or adopting a new trade mark needs to check to ensure that they are not going to run into problems. Many trade mark registers are available online on the Internet, and simple word searching is possible to see if a proposed mark has already been taken by someone else.

You need to check not only whether the exact mark has been registered or applied for earlier by someone else, but whether a similar mark has been. Phonetic equivalents and near equivalents need to be taken into account and searching is not easy. It is particularly difficult in the case of adopting a proposed pictorial mark, as although marks are classified in some Registry systems by way of a classification of so-called 'figurative elements', this is not always applied uniformly.

Professional help

Although it seems simple to register, particularly clearance for use and licensing are areas where it is often better to engage professional assistance from a trade mark attorney. Enforcement may also need professional legal assistance even if the matter does not end up in court. Professionals also have networks of overseas associates enabling all your trade mark portfolio to be handled throughout the world by a single trusted attorney.

Value

Although originally starting up a business or a new product line under a given trade mark does not impart any particular value to the mark itself, once a mark has become established, it becomes a valuable asset in its own right. Indeed, the value of a trade mark registration for a well-known brand may well exceed the tangible value of the entire company promoting that brand. The reason for this is that an established trade mark which is distinctive, well protected by registration, and which has been well policed, provides a substantial 'brand asset' to a third party who may wish to enter the market.

1.4 The essentials of design registration

The law of designs has a long history dating back to the latter part of the eighteenth century. Originally introduced to protect the designing and printing of linens and cottons, design law has been extended over the years to cover functional as well as decorative articles. Designs are applied to a great variety of products from different areas of industry, from complex instruments such as machines, vehicles, engines and architectural structures to simple everyday articles such as clothes, jewellery, toys and furniture.

A design relates to the appearance of the whole or a part of a product, in particular the shape, configuration, pattern or ornamentation. In the UK there are two forms of design protection, registered design provided for by the Registered Designs Act 1949, and design right provided for along principles broadly similar to copyright law.

Design right

Like copyright, design right is subject to qualification requirements and there is no formal registration system. It is not a monopoly right but a right to prevent deliberate copying for a period of 10 years from first marketing of articles made to the design, subject to an overall limit of 15 years from creation. During the last five years, the design right will be subject to licences available as of right, that is the rights holder cannot refuse to sell a licence to others.

For design right to subsist in a design it must be original, not commonplace, and this may apply to the shape or configuration, both internal and external. UK design right does not protect surface pattern or ornamentation.

There is also a community design right, which does not replace the UK system, and gives protection for three years from the date of the first showing to the public.

Design registration

A product's appearance can be crucial to its success, it can help distinguish the goods of one company from those of another, and can provide an important source of revenue. A registered design is a monopoly right protecting the appearance of a product, giving the owner the right to take action against anyone who uses the design without permission. Like other forms of property it can be sold, licensed and exploited to create value and become a financial asset.

To qualify for design registration a design must be new, not identical to another design made available to the public prior to the date of application. However, any disclosure by the designer during the 12 months preceeding the date of application will not compromise novelty. Not only must a design be new, but it must also have individual character, the overall impression it produces must differ from the overall impression of any design which has been made available to the public prior to the application date.

The Registered Designs Regulations 2001 made sweeping changes to design law in order to harmonize the registered designs system in Europe, and the scope of protection has been broadened to incorporate a wide range of products including handicraft items, graphic symbols and typographic typefaces. Designs which are solely dictated by the product's technical function are excluded from registration as are certain emblems and any designs which are immoral or contrary to public policy.

Registration of a design in the UK is a function of the Patent Office and requires illustrations of different views of the design and some information about how the design might be used. Examination usually takes about two months and provided there are no objections, a design will be granted within three to four months of application.

Providing a design registration is renewed every five years, it can last for a maximum of 25 years, that is five periods of five years. The cost of a UK registration is £60 or £35 for a textile for the first five-year period.

Like other areas of intellectual property, design registration is territorial, that is, it will only give protection for the country in which it is filed; for protection abroad it will be necessary to file in the country in which protection is sought. Each country has its own laws and local requirements regarding the procedure for obtaining registration as well as its own definition of what constitutes a registered design.

Under the provisions of an international convention most countries will accept an earlier application as a claim to priority, if the design application is received within six months of the first filing.

While each country has its own national law relating to design registration, there are agreements under which protection can be obtained in a number of countries by making a single application. One example is the Community design right.

In summary:

UK design right:

- automatic, no registration
- copying must be proved
- design must be new and have individual character
- maximum duration 10 years from marketing or 15 from concept
- last 5 years, licence of right

UK design registration:

- a monopoly right – no need to prove copying
- design must be new and have individual character
- 12-month grace period for disclosures made by designer
- application must be filed with the Patent Office
- maximum duration 25 years

Community design right:

- automatic, no registration
- copying must be proved
- design must be new and have individual character
- maximum duration 3 years from date of publication

Community design registration:

- a monopoly right – no need to prove copying
- single registration enforceable in all countries of the European Community
- design must be new and have individual character
- 12-month grace period for disclosures made by designer
- application must be filed with Office for Harmonization in the Internal Market (OHIM)
- maximum duration 25 years

Useful tips for designers

Corner shop or cornered market?
Draw up a business plan to decide on your market (UK, EU, worldwide).

'Patently' a design!
Is it really design registration that you want, or a patent? Get good advice on how many ways you can protect your product.

Can you tell what it is yet?!
Make your application as clear as possible. Your protection is only ever as good as the representations you provide.

Looks that kill
Whenever possible, give it the 'wow' factor. In a competitive market looks can be everything.

Shhhh!
Keep your design a secret until it is registered. Use confidentiality agreements to prevent others from stealing your designs.

Eagle eyes
Take time to research who your competitors are. If they are a serious business, you can be sure they'll know about you.

Possession is 9/10ths of the law

Are you really the owner of your new design? Search as many databases and websites as you can for possible conflicting designs.

I had no idea!

Make sure you know your rights. Look out for seminars on business advice in your area.

Is that it?!

Whenever possible, register the design you intend to market. This may, by now, look quite different from your original representations at the planning stage.

A new European record

Even if you decide not to register, make sure you keep dated records of your design as you may still have unregistered rights, both in the UK and in Europe.

1.5 The essentials of copyright

What is copyright?

Copyright gives the creators of certain kinds of material rights to control ways their material can be used. These rights start as soon as the material is recorded in writing or in any other way. There is no official registration system. The rights cover:

- copying
- adapting
- distributing
- communicating to the public by electronic transmission (including by broadcasting and in an on-demand service);
- renting or lending copies to the public
- performing in public

In many cases, the author will also have the right to be identified on their works and to object if their work is distorted or mutilated.

Before you go any further you need to know that there is no official register for copyright. It is an **unregistered right** (unlike patents, registered designs or trade marks). So, **there is no official action to take** (no application to make, forms to fill in or fees to pay). Copyright comes into effect immediately, as soon as something that can be protected is created and 'fixed' in some way, e.g., on paper, on film, via sound recording, as an electronic record on the Internet, etc.

It is a good idea for you to mark your copyright work with the copyright symbol © followed by your name and the date, to warn others against copying it, but it is not legally necessary in the UK.

The type of works that copyright protects are:

1 Original literary works – for example, novels, newspaper articles, lyrics for songs, and instruction manuals, but not names or titles (these may be registrable as trade marks). Computer programs are also a form of literary work protected by copyright, as are some types of databases.

2 Original dramatic works, including works of dance or mime.

3 Original musical works.

4 Original artistic works – for example, paintings, drawings, engravings, sculptures, photographs, diagrams, collages, maps, technical drawings, logos, works of architecture and works of artistic craftsmanship.

5 Published editions of literary, dramatic or musical works. Protection in this case is of the typographical arrangement of the edition.

6 Films, including videos and digital versatile discs (DVDs).

7 Broadcasts, which may be transmitted by cable or wireless means and including satellite broadcasts, but excluding most transmissions on the Internet.

8 Sound recordings, which may be recordings on any medium, e.g. tape or compact disc, and may be recordings of other copyright works, e.g. musical or literary.

So the above works are protected by copyright, regardless of the medium in which they exist and this includes the Internet. You should also note that **copyright does not protect ideas**. It protects the way the idea is expressed in a piece of work, but it does not protect the idea itself.

How long does UK copyright last?

Copyright in a literary, dramatic, musical or artistic work (including a photograph) lasts until 70 years after the death of the author.

The duration of copyright in a film is 70 years after the death of the last to survive of the principal director, the authors of the screenplay and dialogue, and the composer of any music specially created for the film. Sound recordings are generally protected for 50 years from the year of publication. Broadcasts are protected for 50 years and published editions are protected for 25 years.

For copyright works created outside the UK or another country of the European Economic Area, the term of protection may be shorter. There may also be differences for works created before 1 January 1996.

Are there any exceptions to copyright?

There are a number of exceptions to copyright that allow limited use of copyright works without the permission of the copyright owner. For example, **limited** use of works may be possible for non-commercial research and private study, criticism or review, reporting current events, judicial proceedings, teaching in schools and other educational establishments, not-for-profit playing of sound recordings and to help visually impaired people.

But if you are copying large amounts of material and/or making multiple copies then you may still need permission. Also, particularly where a copyright exception covers publication of excerpts from a copyright work, it is generally necessary to include an acknowledgement. Sometimes more than one exception may apply to the use you are thinking of.

It is important to remember that just owning a copy of a copyright work does not give you permission to use it in a way that would infringe copyright.

If your use of a copyright work does not involve using a substantial part, then you will not be infringing copyright. But it is important to remember that even very small parts of a copyright work may count as a substantial part.

Exceptions to copyright do not generally give you rights to use copyright material; they just state that certain activities do not infringe copyright. So it is possible that an exception could be overridden by a contract you have agreed limiting your ability to do things that would otherwise fall within the scope of an exception.

1.6 The essentials of domain name registration

What is a domain name?

The domain name system (DNS) is not a form of intellectual property, although confusion arises as domain names often work as business identifiers. Essentially though, the DNS helps users to find their way around the Internet.

So a domain name can be similar to a business name and also work as an electronic company address. It is a convenient 'short-hand' way of identifying a company's website address.

Computers connected to the Internet have unique numerical addresses so that electronic information is delivered to the right place. The DNS translates the numerical addresses of computers into more user-friendly names. The resulting domain names are easier to remember and help people to find information on the Internet.

Domain names are used to identify particular web pages. For example, in the website address http://patent.gov.uk the domain name is patent.gov.uk.

Domain names are also used in e-mail addresses, for example, media@patent.gov.uk, that enables people to send and receive electronic messages.

How do I register a domain name?

There are many domain name registrars prepared to register domain names. Each country though has a central register on which to store names and addresses of websites on the Internet.

To register a domain name an application must be made to an accredited domain name registrar.

A list of accredited and accreditation-qualified domain name registrars can be found on the ICANN website (see p. 28).

How do I check if a domain name is available?

In order to check what domain names are available to be registered you can use one of the many domain name registrars' websites.

In the UK Nominet offer a free online search facility – called WHOIS – which enables an enquirer to find out whether a domain name is available and, if not, the organization or person to whom it is registered, and when that registration was made (see p. 28).

The WHOIS will show the following information:

• registrant name
• registrant address (if the opt-out has not been chosen)
• registration agent's name
• registration agent's TAG name
• registration agent's web address
• date of registration
• last time registration was updated
• date renewal is due
• registration status of domain name
• name server information

Renewing your domain name

The renewal date given by the domain name registrars is the next date on which the domain name is due to be renewed (i.e. two years after the original registration or last renewal was made). A renewal fee must be paid before a domain name can be renewed.

In 2003 Nominet introduced the 'positive renewals system'. It allows your registration agents to renew your domain name up to six months in advance of the expiry date. The period between 1 August and 1 November is a 'run-in' period. The positive renewal system can only be used to renew domain names that expire on or after 1 November 2003.

All domain name registrations ending in .uk last for two years from the date of registration. Your domain name certificate will have the expiry date on it or if you don't have your certificate you can check by using the WHOIS facility on the Patent Office's website. Your registration agent will normally contact you before the date your domain name registration expires to ask if you wish to renew it for another two-year period. If for any reason they do not contact you, the Patent Office will contact you once to check whether you would like to renew.

Domain name disputes

Domain name disputes arise largely from the practice of cybersquatting, which involves the pre-emptive registration of trade marks by third parties as domain names. Cybersquatters exploit the first-come, first-served nature of the domain name registration system to register names of trade marks, famous people or businesses with which they have no connection.

Since registration of domain names is relatively simple, cybersquatters can register numerous examples of such names as domain names. As the holders of these registrations, cybersquatters often then put the domain names up for auction, or offer them for sale directly to the company or person involved, at prices far beyond the cost of registration. Alternatively, they can keep the registration and use the name of the person or business associated with that domain name to attract business for their own sites

There are dispute resolution procedures operated, for example, by the World Intellectual Property Organization (WIPO). And if you have a registered trade mark you may have legal remedies against someone who has registered the domain name simply for the purpose of profiting by its sale to the rightful trade mark owner.

As in any legal dispute, it's recommended that you take appropriately qualified legal advice.

Domain names and trade marks

A registration of a domain name does not confer on its owner any trade mark rights and an application to register a domain name as a trade mark must be made to the UK Trade Marks Registry in the normal way, satisfying the requirements of the Trade Marks Act 1994.

Useful websites

ICANN   http://www.icann.org/registrars/accredited-list.html
Nominet http://www.nominet.org.uk/
WIPO   http://www.arbiter.wipo.int/center/index.html

02

intellectual
property and
the business
perspective

In this chapter you will learn:
- about the role of business
  adviser networks
- how a business made money
  from IP
- the value of a patent

2.1 Business adviser networks

The Intellectual Assets Centre – background and function

As part of Scotland's overall ambition for the country to be 'smart and successful'[1] and a leading knowledge economy, the Scottish Executive, in partnership with the Scottish Enterprise and Highlands and Islands Enterprise Networks, launched the Intellectual Assets Centre (IA Centre) in November 2004.

The IA Centre was developed in response to discussions at an intellectual assets (IA) conference at Gleneagles, Scotland in 2001. Despite presenting a little-understood topic, the conference was over-subscribed and follow-up events, one-to-one support and tool development were, thereafter, in constant demand.

This visible market demand was supported by initial studies into the unexploited value of IA in Scottish small and medium-sized enterprises (SMEs) (where estimates of the value of untapped intangible assets in such SMEs ranged from £20 billion to £750 billion).

The IA Centre's remit is to champion and support the issues relating to IA and its importance to Scotland's corporate sector. The Centre achieves these goals by increasing awareness of intellectual assets and by encouraging the demand for, and supply of intellectual asset management (IAM) skills in the Scottish economy. Our aim is to be a centre of excellence and 'the place to go' for impartial expert advice in IAM. With sponsorship from the Scottish Executive and part funding from the European Union the Centre does not act on behalf of any particular commercial interest, its advice is thus unbiased.

The Centre also has the important task of developing Scotland's international profile as a leading exponent of IAM and exploitation. This contributes to the country's ability to attract and retain the best talent and direct foreign investment.

How can the IA Centre help your business?

Our unique value proposition is that we focus on helping businesses to protect/safeguard and exploit the value that lies in the whole range of their intangible assets, not just intellectual property.

[1] *A Smart Successful Scotland*, Scottish Executive (2004).

We make this important discipline accessible through free information, advice and guidance. We do not give grants and do not mentor businesses on a long-term basis. Almost all our interventions are short, some less than half a day, the majority no longer than two days. This means that the time commitment required of our client companies is kept to the minimum.

Our premise is that most businesses have intellectual assets. These can be as simple as your company name or as complicated as a secret process. We think they matter – you might not want to offer them to your customers as products or services but they are still worth something – perhaps a lot – to you (as with Ron Hamilton, as detailed later). Your company might one day want to sell its intellectual assets and you certainly don't want to lose them. So you need to be able to value and protect them properly. At the IA Centre we help Scottish companies do just that.

It's our job to show people with growing businesses how important these 'intangible' businesses can be and how to look after them. We're the first of our kind in the UK, Europe or anywhere.

So what are these intellectual assets? They can be typified as follows:

Brand – what gives your business its distinctive appearance? This will include for instance your name and logo which make up the unique image of your company. It also includes those assets which make other people look favourably on you. They include your business reputation, accreditations and awards that influence people's perception of you.

Intellectual property – what does your business own that is protected by law? This includes assets such as trade marks, patents design rights and copyright that are protected by law.

Innovation – what makes your business's products or services unique? This includes all the ingredients from software and technical drawings to processes and trade secrets that go to make your business's products and services what they are.

Agreements – what value is there in your business's contracts and agreements? For instance all the different kinds of agreement, from franchises to employment contracts.

Networks – what value is there in your contacts and market knowledge. Examples of such assets include databases and service contracts resulting from your knowledge of the market and your relationships with customers and suppliers.

Business processes – what value is there in the way that you are organized? Assets here could include strategies, business plans, along with locations and your connections with other organizations, that makes your business unique.

People – what does your staff know that has value to you? Here, where your people's know-how and experience have been recorded and captured, are assets of your business. (Anything that isn't recorded could leave with your staff and is not an asset.)

How does the IA Centre deliver this help?

- Offering tailored, rather than generic solutions to your business, and signposting you to relevant private and public sector support, as appropriate. Our primary focus is on SMEs, although we also work with organizations of all sizes from the private, voluntary and public sectors. Our advisers come to your location and work with you individually or with your management team.

- Providing tools to answer your questions about IA – why they are important, how you can identify, assess and record your IA, how to manage and ultimately extract additional value from your IA. The Centre's range of tools are available for web-download and free use by your business. These include: information booklets; simulations and games designed to help you more fully understand IA issues; and IA registers and auditing tools. Tool development is ongoing.

- Educating about IA via events, training, seminars and information provision. For instance, events have helped companies to exploit the value in their relationships and in their brands. An international group of experts was brought to Scotland recently to address a major conference looking at articulating the value residing in intangible assets.

- Making accessible a strong portfolio of research activities ranging from case studies examining the ways in which companies have successfully managed their IA to baseline studies and best practice sharing in an international environment.

Working with and contacting the IA Centre

The IA Centre is a subsidiary of Scottish Enterprise and Highlands and Islands Enterprise and has staff, and advisers in both the central belt and the Highlands and Islands. Business Gateway and Local Enterprise Company advisers can help you access the services of the Centre but equally you and your advisers may contact the Centre directly.

Contact details are:

Intellectual Assets Centre®
Suite 6/6 SkyPark
8 Elliot Place
Glasgow G3 8EP

Tel: +44 (0) 141 243 4920
Fax: +44 (0) 141 229 1498
Email: info@ia-centre.org.uk
Web: www.ia-centre.org.uk

2.2 Making money from intellectual property

This section is a case study, showing how Ron Hamilton made money from his intellectual property.

The invention of daily-disposable contact lenses

Making money is never easy and making money from IP is no exception to this rule. You hear of apparently reputable businesses seeking to 'steal' IP because somehow there is less guilt attached to this than taking assets of a more tangible nature. This section explains how my business partner, Bill Seden, and I moved from a small development 'laboratory' in my back garden to a business unit of 6,000 sq. ft in central Scotland in 1993 and how within 3 years the business sold for $33 million in cash with the IP rights selling separately for $15 million. We made money, our public sector investors and the economy made money ... today the business employs 1,200 people in manufacturing in Scotland. IP management was central to this success.

During the 1980s I was employed as vice-president of a major eye-care company. In particular, this company had extensive manufacturing, sales and marketing activities for contact lenses and their cleaning solutions. During that time I was heavily involved in high-volume manufacture of lenses and oversaw the building and commissioning of a solutions manufacturing plant, as it happened, immediately adjacent to one of our most advanced contact lens production facilities. Working closely with me at that time was our technical manager, Bill Seden, and we frequently found ourselves contrasting the way contact lenses were made with the methods adopted for their sister product, cleaning solutions.

In essence, contact lenses were treated as individual items even when made in sizeable batches. The reason for this was that the processes involved were not 'stable', i.e. they gave rise to significant lens-to-lens variation, even when made under 'identical' conditions. The established way to deal with this was to have massive amounts of inspection to weed-out the out-of-tolerance product and to assign parameters to each individual good lens. Process yield was typically 30 per cent. By contrast, making bottles of cleaning solutions relied on strict process control, from the manufacturing environment right through to the selection and mixing process of the various chemicals involved. Process yield was around 100 per cent.

The key question raised by contrasting the processes was, 'if similar disciplines could be applied to the manufacture of contact lenses as are applied to the manufacture of solutions could the cost of making a lens be low enough to render cleaning obsolete?' On the face of it this was a rather idealistic goal. A pair of soft contact lenses retailed at around £150 whereas the cost of cleaning a lens was just a few pence. Only when a similar unit cost could be achieved would substitution be possible. The dream of 'converging' these costs was about to take over the lives of Bill and me.

After some preliminary investigative work at our UK facility I visited the US head office to seek some funding for the formal development of a monthly-disposable contact lens, i.e. one which would be worn continuously for up to 30 days and then thrown away, not cleaned. The conversation went something like this:

'Tell us again Ron what you mean by a disposable contact lens.'
'One which would be worn once and then thrown away.'
'Not cleaned?'
'Never cleaned … single use.'
'Do you know how much money we make from cleaning solutions? Do you know how much we have invested in plant, inventory, etc., etc.?'

These questions were rhetorical ... I had, as mentioned above, just built a cleaning solutions plant and knew only too well the scale of the investments made by the company. The short answer was, 'no budget'.

There were more 'reasoned' objections offered: 'Even if you could reduce the cost of making lenses people would still clean them. We would simply end up selling cheaper lenses. I know, I used to market tooth brushes ... people just don't like throwing things away ... we could not get people to purchase new tooth brushes even when they had worn them down to the handle! Your idea is simply unmarketable'. Some time later when trying to get interest in disposable lenses I was told by a marketing manager for solutions that, 'People *like* cleaning their lenses'.

Unable to raise interest within our company (we even offered to be spun-off and to be arm's length but this was refused) Bill and I resigned in early 1988. The company cars were returned, the pension contributions stopped, the business-class flights stopped and, of course, the salary stopped. It would be wrong to project a 'gung-ho' attitude behind this decision. The fact was that, based on a business plan, we had been offered over £4 million by a leading venture capitalist to start a new business. We had made our intentions clear to our employer and our resignations were accepted in good part.

The funding package was conditional on our 'lead investor' syndicating much of the funding. Preliminary soundings, we were informed, 'indicate that syndication will be easy ... the problem will be deciding which potential co-investors to reject'. But, after making numerous presentations not one company expressed any interest and our lead investor simply walked away! It became clear that had the deal been syndicated our lead investor would have secured an immediate, very large, cash payment and been eligible for 'sweet equity'. However, if it turned out that there was no syndication then they would simply cancel the offer. For them it was a 'win or no loss' formula. We were told that this process was completely legal. Stung by this, I obtained Counsel Opinion which concluded that the withdrawal of the offer of financial facilities was 'in apparent breach of contract'! This opinion was sufficient for me to extract financial redress, just sufficient to cover the cost of some development work and, crucially, the cost of our initial patent application based on this work.

We were, however, about to jump from the frying pan into the fire. Following the above rejection I had contacted a major company regarding our work and, after preliminary discussions, they offered us an option agreement for a full technical appraisal. Fortunately these discussions started after our patent filing had been made (but by only a few days!). We spent several months with their technical teams following which they offered another option. At last there was a chance of seeing our idea funded and a meeting was set up to review the way forward. We went to this meeting convinced that it was to discuss licensing terms and a possible consultancy agreement. The meeting was barely started when a new, to us, representative of the company looked at us and said, 'you two can go now'! Our main contact within the company asked for an adjournment during which he explained to us that his company had calculated that we did not have sufficient financial resources to fund the necessary international patent filing needed to protect our work. It would therefore, shortly, go into the public domain. He explained that they now knew enough to take the technology forward themselves so there was going to be no need to pay us any royalties, which he also explained was completely legal. Lastly, we had insufficient time to find another possible partner ... game, set and match to them!

Having read about the British Technology Group (BTG; then part of the DTI) I asked for a meeting to see if they would be interested in our technology. The upshot of this was that we made an assignment of our patent work in return for a 50/50 share of any related net income secured by BTG. Our patent work was going to be protected even if we had to relinquish it for no immediate payment.

Although BTG was confident that a licence could be secured 'from paper' no such result was achieved even after considerable marketing to contact lens companies worldwide. It was decided that more hard evidence regarding the viability of our process was needed and BTG part-funded a small proof-of-concept laboratory. With the help of some SMART (DTI) money (for related work in contact lenses) we built and proved a small-scale production line complete with 15 ton moulding machine. Once again likely partners in the contact lens industry were contacted by BTG. This time a number visited us but, without exception, they all walked away, each with some plausible explanation on why they were not interested.

It was now four years since we had resigned from employment to start making disposable lenses. Our unit cost goals had been to achieve a level that the lenses would be worn for some 30 days continuously and then destroyed. Evidence was now emerging that overnight wear (sometimes called 'extended' or 'continuous' wear) could result in eye ulcers with potential loss of vision. This wearing modality was now attracting much adverse publicity and the risks, whilst being reduced by not reusing the lens, were still likely to prove a major barrier to the success of our product. It looked like we had reached the end of the road. We had to invent an entirely new concept or give up. If our process could be adapted to produce lenses at an even lower cost threshold than that which was necessary for monthly disposable, we could throw the lenses away after a day ... the idea of daily wear/daily disposable, i.e. no overnight wear, contact lenses was born.

I remember the evening well when I calculated the projected cost of making such a lens, the key was the huge scale-up volumes and the unique stability of our manufacturing 'platform' to deal with these volumes. Without the latter the concept would fail. We calculated that we could make contact lenses such that it would be cost effective to 'wear for a day then throw away'. The labour cost, for example, was below 5 per cent of the best then being achieved, even by heavily automated conventional processes.

After further small-scale tests in 1992 we went public with our invention (*Optician*, 5 June). The article included an endorsement by the department of Optometry at UMIST (the European Centre for Contact Lens Research). This, we thought, will bring them in ... it did not! What *does* it take to be successful in licensing?

Somewhat reluctantly we again decided to try to raise capital to start our own large-scale laboratory. After some difficulty we were able to secure a licence from BTG to make and sell our lenses in Europe. We were able to raise $1 million in equity, mainly from Scottish Enterprise, augmented by government grants. So, after another 12 months of difficult negotiation we opened our first production laboratory in Livingston, Scotland. This was the world's first production facility devoted to making daily-disposable lenses and we had been unable to raise a penny of private sector venture capital.

Inspired by the commercial support of Boots Opticians, who became our major customer, we set about scaling-up the first production line with sales commencing in 1994. In 1995 we were approached by Bausch & Lomb (B & L) for distribution rights. Given the fact that our company, AWARD, was by now established, with demand running ahead of capacity, there was no need for a distributor. However, after a number of meetings we decided to ask B&L if they would like to purchase the business for $33 million in cash ($1 million for every month since starting production). In early 1996 the business was sold for the asking price and another $5 million was made available in incentives to lay the foundations for rapid investment and expansion. B&L also secured a worldwide licence from BTG for $15 million. We had retained 60 per cent of the equity and 50 per cent of the licence income. In 1997 my involvement ended.

Today the company employs 1,200 people in manufacturing (from two in mid 1993). Last year UK output of daily-disposable contact lenses was over 200 million. Perhaps most importantly, daily-disposable contact lens wear, which we had invented and taken to the market, is now regarded as the *safest* and most convenient contact lens wearing modality available.

Conclusion

My experience suggests that making money from IP is not just about the strength of the idea, the technology or the strength of the intellectual property right (IPR). The availability of funding, the cost of protecting IPR and the culture of respect (or lack of it) for the inventor are all factors. To succeed in the UK, where there is, in reality, no early stage venture capital and where the culture is 'if it's legal it's OK' the situation is, to say the least, fraught. Perhaps, ultimately, making money from IP or success in other forms of technology based commercialization requires a personal determination to persist, persist, persist.

03

building your intellectual property

In this chapter you will learn:

- about auditing your IP
- how you can search IP databases
- how and when to license your IP

3.1 The intellectual property audit

In what is increasingly a knowledge-driven economy, intellectual property rights are becoming a key consideration in day-to-day business decisions. Every business uses aspects of intellectual property, it could be in the name it trades under, the process it uses or the products and services it provides. Intellectual property rights are business assets, but unlike most other assets they are more likely to have been neglected because they have not been easy to identify and value.

The intellectual property audit

Finding out what intellectual property you own, and what you do not own, is one of the most reliable ways to reduce risk. A comprehensive audit of this kind may require a team of experts specializing in the various areas of IP, but a simple IP audit can be done by almost anyone if they know what questions to ask.

The 'internal' audit, identifying intellectual property for management purposes. The need here is to focus on the most important areas, and identify:

- Do you have sufficient protection where it matters most?
- Do you have IP that is redundant?
- If others use your IP, what are the terms?
- Do your contracts with employees or subcontractors adequately cover ownership?
- Do you have proper procedures when disclosing confidential information?
- Who owns the IP?

The 'external' audit, identifying third-party IP:

- Do you use or intend to use third-party IP?
- Is the IP properly protected?
- Are proper licensing agreements in place?
- What precisely have you licensed?
- Is it being fully exploited?
- Can you get similar IP free?
- Do you regularly search IP databases?

IP is becoming increasingly important and for any business it is important to know the scope and content of any IP assets the business owns as well as identifying other IP that the business may use or intend to use.

A full audit will include all forms of intellectual property. The trick is to identify what intellectual property exists and how to protect it effectively.

What intellectual property do you own?

Businesses generally spend a lot of time and effort on names, the right name for the business or product could help you stand out from the crowd, the wrong one could place you in a legal dispute. How important is the name of the company, and is it worth protecting it with a registered trade mark? If you have a registered trade mark (RTM) it is worth checking that procedures are in place to ensure that it is kept in force. Never overlook the obvious! One company that recently reviewed its RTM discovered that at the time of a management buy-out all assets were transferred to them, with the exception of the RTM. They were being invoiced for the renewals by the registered owner.

What about product names? A full IP review of the business may uncover other unexploited assets in the form of product names that had not been registered as trade marks, this could leave such products open to abuse by other companies. Perhaps more serious, is the issue of using another company's trade mark without realizing it and thus exposing the company to possible legal action for infringement.

Have you any patented technology? If so it is important that it is kept in force, renewals will have to be paid annually, if not the patent will lapse and become available for anyone to use. If you are not using the technology it will be worthwhile exploring the possibility of licensing it to others. Businesses must always seek to maximize the value extracted from IP; if it is not used and there is no likelihood of licensing you must review.

Do you license in any technology? If so check the agreement and establish just what it is you have licensed. One company recently discovered that the licensing agreement it had entered into was on the basis of the certificate of grant, and it said absolutely nothing about the extent of the patent! It had already spent a considerable amount of money in preparing the production process.

Promoting any business is important. One company in particular found copyright ownership a very important issue when it did an audit. The company has a number of prestigious clients and had engaged the services of a professional production company to produce a video of some of its work for these clients. This was an important asset for the company, but unfortunately it did not own the work. It was a work protected by copyright and the contractor, in this case the production company, retained copyright ownership. Unauthorized use by the company could result in trouble.

A trade mark audit

This should include:

- identification of someone to take responsibility for trade mark issues
- avoidance of descriptive names
- proper procedures for the registration and renewals processes
- an assessment of future plans and product
- discovery and recording of unregistered marks
- review of any licensing agreements
- regular review of trade mark portfolio
- regular trade mark searches to monitor legitimate usage

A patent audit

This should include:

- identification of someone to take responsibility for patent issues
- proper records of technical developments for assessment
- records of patents held and filed
- procedures for renewal
- regular review of patent portfolio including licensing arrangements
- confidentiality review
- regular search of patents relevant to business activity

The copyright audit

This should include:

- adoption of best practice by affixing copyright notices
- identifying and recording copyright of commercial value
- establishment of ownership
- review of licensing agreements

The design audit

This should include:

- identification of someone to take responsibility for design issues
- records of designs held and filed
- procedures for renewal
- regular review of design portfolio including licensing arrangements
- regular search of designs relevant to business activity

These lists are in no way exhaustive but serve to cover the kind of issues that may be relevant to the business. In conducting and establishing an audit process it is important to identify what is to be accomplished and to make sure that this is achieved. It is also important to record the entire process.

The record should include the objective, the plan and how it was executed. It should describe and evaluate the intellectual property issues and propose recommendations for improvements with a timescale for review. It goes without saying that the audit should be treated as commercially sensitive.

Doing nothing

Focusing on issues such as these is the first stage in working out an IP strategy that fits your business best. A regular review of IP is far more desirable, and a lot easier, than putting it off until something happens that forces you to look at it. If left unprotected, your intellectual property rights may be lost to those that are better placed to commercialize them leaving your business without any financial gain. A simple audit is a good place to start, recognizing your IP and taking adequate steps to protect it should enable you to take advantage of the IPR system and profit from your creativity. Good, regular management of IP is even better.

Examples of the IP audit in practice – service industry

GreenGrass International plc

Patents

The company was clearly aware of patents as a means of protection. It had previously been granted a patent on machinery used in the laying of turf. This patent had subsequently been sold to a third party. The company was also active in the development of turf cutting and rolling machines and had recently developed a new machine which was believed to incorporate novel features.

If the machine is in any way novel then patenting is an option. However, if any technical aspect of those novel features was to be disclosed prior to filing then that feature, once disclosed, could not be patented. A clear danger would arise if the machine was to be placed in any exhibition, which was the intention. Professional advice should always be sought on the issue of patenting. The cost of obtaining patent protection can be expensive and there can be little point in obtaining a patent if the effective tools to enforce the patent are not available.

Another issue is that of ownership. GreenGrass International plc has designed the new features but is not manufacturing the machine. If the manufacturer suggests any further improvements, ownership of any resulting IP must be agreed. It is recommended that agreements be made before any collaboration process begins. It is also good practice to deal with third parties such as this only on the basis of written confidentiality agreements in order to prevent the disclosure of the invention.

Designs

The company had not previously considered registered designs as relevant to its business. However, it had developed and used a system of 'turf tiles' to repair damaged areas of turf. There existed the possibility that future developments of the trays for these 'tiles' may contain unique elements in their appearance which could be protected by a registered design.

Trade marks

The company currently owns one registered trade mark, covering two classes, class 31 turf and class 42 professional consultancy services relating to the grass turf industry. There also exists at least one product 'Flite turf' which might also be protected by registration. Though 'Flite turf', if it's a known technical term in the turf industry may be too descriptive, there was the option of registration in the same distinctive style as the other registered marks. If a trade mark is not registered it is an offence to use ®, however ™ can be used to indicate a trade mark irrespective of whether it has been registered or not.

Copyright

Copyright protects literary, artistic, musical and dramatic works. Any brochures, promotional material, etc. are automatically protected by copyright. The important issue here is that of ownership. The paying of money does not automatically transfer the rights to the commissioner. In the case of any material produced by a subcontractor then ownership will remain with the subcontractor unless there is an explicit agreement to the contrary. Ownership of the copyright in the promotional mini disk ownership rests with the creator. Contained on that disk, and on the video produced, is footage of work being carried out at a Premier League football ground. Even though the company paid the football club monies for permission to film, the subcontractor owns copyright in that piece of film. If it is to be used elsewhere the copyright owner will have to give permission for use and will be entitled to additional payment. In any contract the commissioners of the work should always attempt to have all intellectual property rights assigned to them.

Examples of the IP audit in practice – software industry

RollDigi Ltd

The main area of business activity relates to: the design, manufacture and development of hardware and software; rugged equipment for harsh environments; software for process interfacing; and printed circuit design and supply.

Patents

The company was aware of patents as a means of protection and had lodged a number of patent applications. Only one patent application appears on the public database, GB1234567, a patent application for the 'Erasure of Recording Media', the application was terminated before grant.

From discussions it would seem that the company has adopted a strategy of filing applications, but not proceeding to grant. A strategy which seems to have succeeded in its intention of putting competitors on notice of the new technology, and using the time gained to build on its first-to-market strategy. This illustrates a keen awareness of one of the ways the patent system can be used to gain competitive advantage, without actually having to proceed down the expensive route of having the patent granted.

However, this strategy is not without risk and would not afford any exclusive rights; the opportunity to license successful technology would be lost. There are opportunities to patent and these opportunities should be considered.

Software can be patented, provided there is a so-called technical effect. This technical effect can take place either within the computer itself, making, say, more effective use of the computer's memory and thus enabling the hardware represented by the computer itself to work in a technically improved way; or it can be external to the computer by increasing, say, the efficiency with which an attached device – such as a robotic arm – can be used.

As well as software some of the elements on the rugged equipment under development might also be considered patentable.

Patent protection can be an expensive process and the company should ensure that it capitalizes on the technology. If the technology is not being used, an option available would be to license out the technology to a third party. An important issue to consider in any collaborative venture such as this, is that of ownership. If a third party was to suggest any improvements or modifications to the patent then the ownership of any resulting IP must be agreed. It is recommended that agreements be made before any collaboration process begins. It is also good practice to deal with third parties such as this only on the basis of written confidentiality agreements in order to prevent the disclosure of any subsequent IP.

The cost of obtaining patent protection can be expensive and there can be little point in obtaining a patent if the effective tools to enforce the patent are not available.

Trade marks

The company has a number of registered trade marks covering classes 09, 37 and 42. The proprietor is given as RollDigi Limited, however, the address on the trade mark database is shown as 21–30 Oaktree Road, Clifton, Bristol. The Patent Office records may need to be amended to reflect the current address.

Trade marks can be an important marketing tool and are intended to act as a 'badge of origin'. As such the mark could be applied to all RollDigi products to highlight their origin. The registered trade mark symbol could be used.

Copyright

In the case of software produced by the company, the act of recording that software automatically attracts copyright. Recording may take any form be it in writing or simply storing it electronically on disk or incorporated into hardware.

Copyright protection is free but it will only protect against copying, translation, adaptation and rearrangement. Copyright also does not prevent someone else developing and marketing a competing product by using your novel idea, as long as they do not directly copy. Patents by contrast can protect the inventive concepts underlying the creation of a new program.

It is advisable to display prominent copyright notices on the versions of software you sell to end-users. The notice should say '© [name] [year] all rights reserved'. You can also ask that users of your software sign an 'end-user's licence' before they use it. In such a licence you can set the terms under which people use your software, including what uses are permissible. This is an area where specialist legal advice should be sought.

Audits in practice – manufacturing industry

CircleRide Ltd

The main area of business activity relates to: the design, manufacture and development of axles, suspension units, loading systems and couplings for trailers.

Patents

The company was aware of patents as a means of protection and had lodged at least two European Patent Applications. EP 1234567 ceased on 6.04.99 and the other EP 2345678 ceased on 6.04.99. With these patents it was interesting to note the difference in the number of designated states, the former had four designations the latter 13. The more states covered the greater the cost, possible markets should be carefully considered against the costs of protection.

The company has in the past employed the services of a patent agent to handle all its patent applications and as such there are no concerns relating to patent protection. However, it is worth pointing out that there were some concerns over the disclosing of information before a patent was filed. Any disclosure to a third party could have disastrous implications when considering the novelty of the invention: an invention will lack novelty if it has been disclosed.

It is also important to establish ownership when working with third parties. If a third party was to suggest any improvements or modifications to the patent then the ownership of any resulting IP must be agreed. It is recommended that agreements be made before any collaboration process begins. It is also good practice to deal with third parties, such as this, only on the basis of written confidentiality agreements in order to prevent the disclosure of any subsequent IP.

Patent protection can be an expensive process and the company should ensure that it capitalizes on the technology. If the technology is not being used, an option available would be to license out the technology to a third party. The cost of obtaining patent protection can be expensive and there can be little point in obtaining a patent if the effective tools to enforce the patent are not available.

It should be pointed out that as well as the protection offered by patents there is also a great deal of commercial and technical information stored in patent documents. This can play a significant role in a broad range of business activities: from basic research through to product marketing. Before research projects are initiated, a scan of the published literature to establish what is already known can save many hours pursuing fruitless lines of investigation.

Trade marks

The company have two registered trade marks covering classes 12 and 17. However, the proprietor is given as Circle Rubbers Ltd, New Road, Penrith, Cumbria. It is understood that this reflects the original trade mark owners, prior to the management buy-out. It is important that the register reflects the true owners, so this issue should be addressed as soon as possible. The Patent Office records may need to be amended to reflect the current owners.

3.2 Searching intellectual property databases

IP databases contain a wealth of commercial and technical information, which for the most part is free to access. The most common reason for a business to search databases for registered designs or registered trade marks would be to establish possible infringement problems. These could range from the business seeking to consider what designs or trade marks of its own could potentially conflict with existing rights, or perhaps the business wishes to monitor new applications coming onto the register which pose a potential threat to its own existing registered rights. Publicly available trade mark and designs databases, and how to use them to best effect, will be discussed later in this section.

With patents the motivation to search goes beyond simply detecting infringement risks, either by the business against the granted patents of rivals, or by rivals against the business's own patents. It is far more common for patent databases to be searched for a variety of other reasons, which could include:

- to understand the state-of-the-art in a particular technology
- to benefit from previous research made by others, thereby saving repeated effort
- to seek technology to license in as a cheaper solution to a problem than a home-made invention
- to seek partners to whom a business's own patents could be licensed out
- to understand the direction of competitors' current research, to determine future challenges in the market or potential opportunities to license out or license in
- to find potential customers for the business's own products, or find potential suppliers of relevant products

In fact, the list goes on and on!

The modern patent system is based on the assumption that in exchange for a short-lived exclusive right to a technology, said technology will be disclosed for the public to read and understand (it was not always so!). For this reason patent databases are well ordered, updated weekly or even daily and contain a goldmine of information.

Free patent searching – *esp@cenet* ®

The *esp@cenet* database, maintained by the European Patent Office (EPO) is a major achievement in international cooperation. It contains patent collections from the EPO itself, the national patent offices of the European Patent Organization, the United States Patent and Trademark Office, the Japanese Patent Office, the World Intellectual Property Organization (i.e. international applications under the Patent Cooperation Treaty (PCT)) and several other major patent offices. In total, the collection is fast approaching over 60 million patents from more than 70 patent granting authorities.

The database can be accessed via the websites of the national patent offices of the European Patent Organization (the so-called national gateways), or via the EPO website itself.[1] Unless a user already knows the particular patent number he or she is looking for, it is the 'Advanced' search query page where most enquiries are made. This search 'form' includes a tips and advice tool called the '*esp@cenet* assistant' which can be consulted at any stage of the search to help users phrase their enquiry correctly and to understand (and sift) the resulting documents. At whichever stage of a search a user might get into difficulty, the assistant proffers relevant hints and helpful error messages.

The advanced search form has ten searchable fields, which can be used in combination. Some of the search fields are self-explanatory, like the name of the inventor. If you type in a name the resulting hit-list will show the titles of all patents which have that name as an inventor. Typing in the name of the applicant (i.e. the inventor's employer or some other company name) can often bring unexpected results. In this case, it is best to make sure that you know the legal name of the company (as would appear on, e.g., patent documents) in addition to whatever familiar brand it uses in the marketplace. (For example, the patent applicant for 'L'Oréal®' cosmetic products would, in fact, be Oreal.)

If you are fortunate enough to know the serial number of the patent you are looking for, you could, of course, just search for that number. This assumes that you can get two things right. Firstly, you have to know if the number you have is the application number (assigned to the application when it was filed at the respective national or regional patent office) or the publication number under which it was published, often up to 18 months after its first filing date.

[1] http://ep.espacenet.com/

Secondly, you have to be sure that the number you have is expressed in the correct format for the database to recognize it. The recommendation here is to do a crude search and look at the way in which patent numbers (both application and publication) are expressed on documents from the territory of interest. Armed with concrete examples of the format protocols for the country in question, a search can then be performed in confidence.

For searchers performing a state-of-the-art search, they will be interested in combining keywords for specific technical features with classification codes which limit the search to particular technical areas. These make for extremely potent searches and the proper use of classification codes cannot be over-emphasized.

The search field 'keywords in title or abstract' accepts regular English language inputs, with 'wildcard' truncation (*) and Boolean operators like AND or OR or NOT. But searching on keywords which might appear in the titles or abstracts (which may vary in length from 100 to 200 words) of target patent documents is not the most efficient way to retrieve the most relevant documents.

Patent classification schemes

In addition to any national classification scheme applied to patents by a national patent office to its own documents, all published patents are also classified according to the International Patent Classification[2] scheme, bearing at least one, but often more, codes which denote the technologies to which the patent relates. For example, under this scheme, all footwear patents (whether for shoes and boots, methods of their manufacture or machinery therefor) are classified under A43. Further fine subdivisions in this area bring us to A43B (footwear), A43B5 (sports footwear) and A43B5/02 (football boots).

So, were you wishing to find all published patents relating to football boots with releasable studs, you could enter 'A43B5/02' in the IPC search field and 'stud' in the field for keywords in title or abstract. Combinations could also be tried for 'stud AND releas*'. Note here how the truncated term 'releas*' encompasses occurrences in the abstract of 'released', 'releases', 'releasing', 'releasably', etc. It is also worth considering all the other words by which a releasable part might be described: detachable, dismountable, removable, (dis)connectable, etc.

[2] http://www.wipo.int/classifications/ipc/ipc8/?lang=en the current edition of the IPC is edition 8 (since January 2006)

What might also interest you would be that features of shoe or boot studs *per se* are classified under A43C15/16, so it is likely that for those patents in which the invention relates to the stud of a football boot, it would be worth running a search against 'A43B5/02 AND A43C15/16' or perhaps 'A43B5/02 OR A43C15/16' as a Boolean combination. This could further be refined with keyword searches for 'releas* AND detach* AND dismount*', etc. Note that the latter IPC code covers the notion of studs, so this word would not need to be included in the keyword search. Indeed, by using IPC codes which encompass as much as possible the nature of the target invention, you can use the keywords to focus on a very specific aspect.

The European Patent Office uses a patent classification system of its own, based heavily on the IPC, called ECLA. In a great many instances the IPC and ECLA codes for a particular invention are the same, except that the ECLA code will have additional characters on its right to indicate yet further fine subdivisions of the corresponding IPC code. Looking at A43C15/16 (studs for shoes and boots, e.g. football boots) once again, you will find that in ECLA this classification has been further subdivided as follows:

- A43C15/16 studs (or cleats) for football or like boots
- A43C15/16A characterized by attachment to the sole
- A43C15/16C characterized by the shape
- A43C15/16C1 having a circular cross-section
- A43C15/16C1A pointed or conical, e.g. calks, spikes or pins
- A43C15/16C1B frusto-conical or cylindrical
- A43C15/16R with resilient means, e.g. shock absorbing means

From this it becomes clear that a search using A43C15/16A in the ECLA field would be even more effective at retrieving the sort of documents of interest to us (namely boots with releasable studs).

Whilst all EP patents have both IPC and ECLA codes within *esp@cenet*, a great many other non-EP documents have also been classified under ECLA too. This means that this refined classification scheme can be used when searching most documents from Europe and indeed, across the world.

Once you have a hit-list of documents corresponding to your search criteria you can start to go through it, document by document. Firstly you will be able to see bibliographic data on the patent, like who the applicant and inventor were; when it was filed and published; and crucially where it was classified.

Often the IPC and ECLA codes on documents retrieved in your first search suggest other areas of the classification scheme to which you should turn your attention.

Also worth a look are the other documents cited against the patent in question. These can be found on the front page of granted US patents, or on the back pages of most other patent applications (e.g. GB, EP, WO) in the 'search report'. If the document you are looking at is of relevance to your enquiry, then the documents cited against it are likely to interest you too: so go and look them up. And when you do – again enquire as to where they were classified and what was cited against them. And so on.

'Family matching' and legal status

You can also cross-reference the patent in question so as to bring up its 'family members' and its legal status. The 'simple' family can be accessed through the 'also published as' function in *esp@cenet*; and the 'extended' family can be accessed through the 'view INPADOC patent family' link. By 'family' we usually mean all those patent filings in various countries sharing a priority document. An initial filing in the USA, for example, can be the basis of patent filings across the world – but the serial number of the US priority document will enable them all to be linked as relating to the same invention. Only family members which have been granted in territories where you might be wishing to trade pose a potential problem if your technology is similar. The current status of the application and its family can be checked too, e.g. if it has been examined or granted yet.

National patent office databases can also confirm the legal status of patents in their own territory. For example, in the UK the 'Patent Status Information Service'[3] will tell you if a patent has been granted, whether or not it is being renewed to be kept in force, if it has lapsed or if its ownership has changed. This covers both GB patents and those EP patents which designate UK.

Furthermore, for those who wish to avidly track the progress of a published European patent application as it goes through the examination process there is an 'On-Line File Inspection'[4] service. All correspondence on the application file, e.g. between the examiner and the attorney, has been scanned and made available.

[3] http://webdb4.patent.gov.uk/patents
[4] http://www.epoline.org/portal/public/registerplus

This enables third parties to see what arguments are being made both for and against the application, giving an indication as to the likely form of the granted claims. This means that third parties can submit their own arguments prior to grant, or prepare their own opposition arguments ready for use immediately after grant.

Reasons to search

It is worth remembering that searches differ according to their purpose. When a patent examiner is searching a new patent application, he or she is comparing the technical disclosures in the description of earlier patents applications (and other documents) against the claims of the application in question. This is a 'novelty' search. Sometimes these will be done to check the validity of a patent, which is either being offered for sale or license, or which is being enforced. In such circumstances the searcher wants to know what prior art might be out there that could possibly destroy the patent.

Similar to a 'novelty' search is a general 'state-of-the-art' search, which aims to bring up all documents disclosing particular features as defined either in a draft claim or in some other parameters defined by a client. Often such searches are done as a 'patent watching' service, conducted regularly to monitor new patent applications in a particular technology area of interest to a client who is concerned about new developments from rivals.

Infringement searches and 'freedom to operate' searches, on the other hand, are concerned with the granted claims of a patent which is in force in a relevant territory when compared with a particular product or process which a party might be carrying out. Unlike a novelty search (where considerations of novelty are global) the searcher can ignore patents from other territories. However, it is the content of the granted claims of the target documents which must be studied, rather than their descriptions, as the searcher is trying to establish 'does product or process X infringe any rights in this territory?'

Other sources of patent searching services

Extra help in search matters can be obtained from a variety of sources. The so-called PATLIB centres[5] can be found in many European cities, sometimes on university campuses, otherwise in public libraries. There are over a dozen in the UK. The website or call centres of national patent offices can usually assist with basic enquiries too (e.g. vexations over patent number formats). The EPO provides training courses on basic and advanced *esp@cenet* searching throughout the year and details can be found on the EPO's patent information website.[6]

National patent offices and a variety of specialist commercial patent information providers can offer a range of 'value-added' search services above and beyond the free information in, for example, *esp@cenet*. Whilst free and paid-for patent databases have similar content (namely complete classified collections of national and regional patents), the functionality and sophistication of their search tools differs quite considerably. Some also permit extensive searching in non-patent literature, e.g. academic journals. Most will also offer to conduct your search for you, at a premium, if you would prefer a professional to dive into the sea of information on your behalf.

More information on patents is provided in Sections 1.2, 3.3, 5.1, 6.1 and 6.2.

Trade mark databases

By comparison with patents, trade mark searching is comparatively quick and simple.

National patent office websites typically have trade mark databases for their own national collections.[7] A searcher will need to check the national databases in the markets in question, the European Community Trade Mark (CTM) database at OHIM[8] and the Madrid system trade mark database at WIPO for pending international applications.[9] In most cases this is just a simple matter of typing in the text of the proposed trade mark and seeing if the resulting hits are registered in classes of good or services which are likely to cause conflict.

[5] http://patlib.european-patent-office.org/

[6] For information on training, visit the Learning Centre at http://patentinfo.european-patent-office.org/

[7] For example, the UK Patent Office's Trade Marks Register can be found here: http://www.patent.gov.uk/tm/t-find-text.htm, within which one would normally make a 'mark text' search

[8] See OHIM's 'CTM-Online' database at http://oami.europa.eu/

[9] See more information on the Madrid system (http://www.wipo.int/madrid/en/) at the World Intellectual Property Organization; the database can be found here: http://www.wipo.int/madrid/en/services/madrid_express.htm

In addition to information on who owns a trade mark (or an application therefor), their contact details, and the classes of trade to which it relates (see below), the databases will tell you if an application is withdrawn, terminated, pending, examined, registered or being opposed. The database will also indicate what type of mark it is – whether it is just the text itself, or the text limited to some specially stylized format (i.e. the word is protected only when in a particular font), or when the text is used in or with a logo (a so-called 'device' mark) – in which latter case the database should also have an image on file to be consulted.

Trade mark classifications

Like patents, trade marks are classified according to an international scheme, named after the French town of Nice[10] where the treaty establishing the scheme was concluded. The scheme comprises 45 principal areas of commercial activity for goods and services, and a trade mark owner can seek to have their mark registered in one or more of these areas. This system permits identical marks to co-exist on a register if they are in differing areas of trade. Compare, for example, 'Lotus' registered to different owners for:

- cars (class 12)
- shoes (class 25)
- computers and software (class 9)

A trade mark owner's rights are limited to the classes of trade within which their mark is registered.

Reasons to search trade marks

Before trading in goods or services in any territory, it is essential to check what similar rights might already exist for the name, logo or brand on your offerings. You might also spot an opportunity to register rights of your own.

---

[10] More information on the Nice classification can be seen here: http://www.wipo.int/classifications/nice/en/, and the listing for the 45 classes can be seen here:
http://www.wipo.int/classifications/fulltext/nice8/enmain.htm

You will also be wanting to monitor new applications coming onto the registers which may be harmful to the distinctiveness of your own mark were they to be allowed to proceed to registration. In many jurisdictions it is often the case that the burden of objecting to new applications falls heavily on the existing rights owners. In such circumstances, it is advisable to consult a trade mark attorney to decide how to respond to new applications for marks from potential rivals.

As is the case with patents there are commercial trade marks database providers and their added-value services typically include 'watching' services to monitor databases around the world for new applications which are a potential conflict to a client's existing marks.

More information on trade marks is provided in Sections 1.3, 5.2, 6.3 and 6.4.

Registered designs databases

The designs registers at national patent offices[11] or at OHIM[12] give users quick access to thousands of images of existing designs. As with trade marks, this gives a user the chance to determine what existing rights are already registered in a particular territory and alerts a user to new rights coming onto the register for which an existing rights owner might need to make a response. Note that OHIM has been administering a Community-wide design registration system since 2003.

Designs classification

Under European law the enforceability of designs is no longer limited to the classes by which they are indexed, but nevertheless the classification system is still applied to facilitate searching. The Locarno classification scheme,[13] named after the Swiss town in which the treaty was concluded, is used by over 40 countries.

---

[11] For example, an 'image' search at the UK Patent Office: http://www.patent.gov.uk/design/dbase/index.htm

[12] http://oami.europa.eu/en/design/default.htm

[13] More information on the Locarno scheme can be seen on the WIPO website: http://www.wipo.int/classifications/locarno/en/. The scheme itself is here: http://www.wipo.int/classifications/fulltext/locarno8/enmn01.htm

The Locarno classification scheme comprises 31 main classes (and a 'miscellaneous' class) for particular types of products, and these are subdivided yet further, for example:

Class or subclass	Design
Class 21	games, toys, tents and sports goods
Subclass 01	games and toys
Sub-subclass D0205	dolls

A typical designs database will allow a user to search for designs in a particular Locarno class or subclass and/or for designs belonging to a particular proprietor. As you would expect, each entry on the register leads you to all the relevant images on file, plus information on the proprietor of the right, and the legal status of the registration.

More information on registered designs is provided in Sections 1.4, 5.3 and 6.5.

3.3 Licensing your intellectual property

Introduction: due diligence, valuation and ground work

At the start of 2005, 99.3 per cent of UK business enterprises were small (0–49 employees) and 0.6 per cent medium (50–249 employees). SMEs represent a significant area of growth for the UK and technology. Patents and intellectual property (IP) should be at their foundation and play a key role in determining SME business strategy. Many SMEs manage their patents with diligence and skill but too many companies fail to realize the power of the licensing process and the potential economic reward to be gained when these assets are well managed.

What is a licence?

Essentially a licence in its simplest form is a permission to do something (manufacture or have manufactured by others, market and sell), something (a product, process, know how etc.) that could otherwise be legally restrained. The licence is agreed between the licensor (source of the invention) to the licensee. In recent years licensing has become a major contributor to economic growth in the US and in parts of Europe, and without doubt China is rapidly catching up.

Your company can only benefit from a thorough understanding of its IP and a policy that recognizes that diligent IP management is required to successfully commercialize technology and products via licensing.

To understand the vocabulary used by patent agents, IP lawyers and business development consultants engaged in the business of IP management is daunting to the uninitiated. Many companies fail to grasp this basic understanding and will continue pouring money into products that can't be patented and research that has already been undertaken by others and will constitute prior art so preventing them from fully or legally commercializing that research.

Common mistakes

SMEs need to think about IP in terms of value and to see that the value vested in the patent or IP portfolio probably accounts for the core value in the company. This value does not stand still, once created it must be recognized, managed and extracted.

For companies who are new to licensing and can't afford or do not wish to take professional advice, the complexity involved and the many hats required to stay the course may generate mistakes. It is, though, deeply sad when companies lose value or commercial reputation when they fail to take what could be a simple step, if only they had known.

Companies may fail to:

• Recognize the potential value vested in the IP.
• Understand that filing a UK patent application does not provide instant world-wide protection.
• Appreciate that inventors as named in the patent must be genuine inventors rather than a director wanting to share in the fame and glory.
• Appreciate the basic legal foundation that underpins all aspects of IP – if you don't follow the rules you may end up in court.
• Remember that the patent portfolio should protect the product being commercialized – it sounds obvious but you would be surprised at how inventors lose sight of the objective.
• Ensure full right of ownership when the SME is, for instance, based on university-derived IP.

- Understand the need for confidentiality and how failure to maintain confidentiality can lose them the patent, trade secrets, market credibility and potential value in the company.
- Recognize and record copyright.
- Include IP ownership guidelines and the need for confidentiality within employee contracts of employment.
- Create dated, signed (ideally witnessed) paper trails that others (licensees, a court or new owner if the company is sold) will be able to follow in all dealings concerning inventions, patents and IP commercialization.
- Recognize the need to fully research all existing patents filed in their market sector before making financial commitments to that market.
- Enter into clear, legally binding agreements regarding ownership rights before entering into joint research, product development collaborations and financing agreements with other companies and individuals.
- Be prepared to fully understand the real needs of their potential licensee. It is difficult to sell a new product without understanding the needs of the potential buyer – licensing is exactly the same.
- Ensure that all decision makers, including inventors, are aware of and supportive of the company entering into license negotiation.
- Obtain an independent valuation in the acquisition of a company with an asset or patent portfolio.
- Budget adequately for the costs and time involved in filing patents in all major markets across the world. It is critical to file accurate claims and this may take time.
- Appreciate that your normal 'business lawyer' will probably not be a specialist IP lawyer.
- Appreciate that if you own patents you must be prepared to defend them – this requires time, money, IP lawyers and nerves of steel.

Why carry out due diligence?

In order to really appreciate the value and strength vested in your IP it is essential to carry out a few basic steps of due diligence; only then will you really hold the information necessary to enter into any form of valuable licensing negotiation. It is not good business practice to leave the due diligence to the other party; the licensor must enter the negotiation understanding all the benefits and risks regarding the IP to be commercialized.

It is worth noting that this same information will be required if you wish to successfully raise finance, sell your business or the IP and if you enter into various forms of research and development collaboration. To enter into these business development processes without having carried out due diligence will put you in risk of losing your patents, your financial edge and your reputation in the marketplace.

Any credible licensee should also undertake the same due diligence that you should have carried out. If you are considering entering into negotiation with a potential licensee you would expect any serious company to come to the table armed with as much information as possible about your company and your products. Licensing out to another company means that you are entering into what should be a long-term mutually profitable partnership and like any form of relationship building it would normally progress via a series of specific steps. These steps will vary slightly within different business sectors but will generally develop along the following lines when the licensor is looking to find a licensee. The licensor (source of the invention/IP):

1 Carries out an IP audit analysis in order to understand the commercial strengths and weaknesses of their own portfolio.
2 Undertakes due diligence.
3 Determines IP strategy by market sector, geographic territory etc.
4 Identifies potential partners.
5 Approaches potential partners with non-confidential information.
6 May carry out meetings to discuss only non-confidential details with selected potential partners.

At this stage the potential licensee will start to carry out their own due diligence on the potential licensor and their IP. Companies involved in technologies such as biotechnology and healthcare will experience the added risk and complication that their IP is evolving as the negotiations progress.

7 Licensor enters into a Confidentiality Agreement (CDA) or Non Disclosure Agreement (NDA) with serious and appropriate potential licensees.

8 Licensor carries out its own analysis of the potential licensee's credit rating, history, own product quality etc.

9 Licensor forwards the confidential information package to the potential licensee and can enter into more serious and open meetings and set the base for negotiation.

The potential licensee should now be carrying out an in-depth due diligence exercise. The outcome may lead to requests from the licensee for any of the following: further discussion and negotiation, an Evaluation agreement, a Material Transfer Agreement (MTA), an Option Agreement (this may be Exclusive or Non Exclusive in the territory under negotiation), disclosure of information not yet provided or, of course, they may decide to walk away.

10 If the licensee wishes to continue then the licensor needs to ensure that there is agreement or 'buy-in' for this process throughout the company. In an ideal world it's best to also ensure that the potential licensee has 'buy-in' to this partnership throughout their company.

11 At this stage the licensor needs to be trying to review financial and patent data for the licensee and where possible, gain access to data concerning any past commercial collaborations that they have entered into; the gossip in the community can be useful.

From this point both parties should have entered into serious negotiation that involves their IP lawyers and that establishes at least an outline of the licence terms acceptable to both.

Aims

Licensing generally takes products into foreign markets more quickly than would otherwise be possible and reduces the legal and financial risks taken by the SME licensor. You will not have to cope with export barriers, your licensing agreements should hold a degree of flexibility but you may lose some control in return for financial gain. Licensing generates return on investment while the licensor can move forward with in-house development of future products to be out licensed; it adds strength to the licensor's market position, helps prevent copying of the IP and helps build a positive market image.

Understanding risk and reward

The due diligence exercise will result in a more thorough understanding of the real and potential risk factors and the potential rewards; this will help the licensor to knowledgeably build partnering plans.

Due diligence steps

The due diligence exercise provides the licensor with a health check that should be carried out and recorded on a regular basis. This groundwork supports the partnering process and will be used not only through the negotiation process but also in making many business development decisions and, if need arises, in pursuing potential infringers.

Market

This is not straightforward where the technology is entirely new and in this case it may be advisable to seek expert help.

- This should include market sector value, market forecasts and a review of return on investment.
- Review the existing and potential competitive position together with all factors that influence this market.
- Review changes, trends, market dynamics and problems, such as safety issues in the market.
- Review any likely regulatory changes on a country-by-country basis (this especially applies to the healthcare market).
- The route to market should include an analysis of the most cost-effective methods of manufacture and sale, incorporating the distribution or take-to-market chain. You should arrive at a picture of access, costs and time scales.

Competition

- A review of competitive companies, their costs, reputation, success and product range, strength in the market and also those companies trying to access the market.
- A comparison of your technology against the competition.

IP and patent

- Identify exactly what will be transferred or partnered.
- Ensure that all ownership rights have been transferred to the licensee (there may have been early stage design help where no agreements were in place or IP may have been transferred from a university where the inventors had not assigned their rights).
- The licensor needs to ensure that they have not entered into any earlier agreements that may prevent other partnering transactions from taking place.
- Licensor needs to ensure that there are no third-party rights that will prevent commercialization of their IP.

- Ensure that all patents and other intellectual assets are current and fully maintained; check the status of patent searches and examinations.
- Ensure that you are aware of any ongoing litigation that may affect your IP rights.

Scientific (where relevant)

This should include time frames and costs that will be involved in regulatory trials, meeting statutory requirements and regulatory requirements in all relevant countries. This may need to include a review of any other patents that will need to be accessed in order to fully develop the technology.

IP valuation

Valuation may be undertaken as a tax reference point prior to commercialization or as part of the due diligence partnering exercise or prior to seeking funding. Many complex models exist but at the initial due diligence stage it should be sufficient to bench mark your technology against existing deals where they exist, to build discounted cash flow (DCF) models (incorporating the risk factors that you have identified earlier in the due diligence process) and to build a net present value (NPV) model. NPV is really just the sum of the licensor's expected cash flow discounted by the cost of the capital involved. There are many occasions when complex valuations are required but the essential need here is to have a justifiable and sensible financial data package to back up your negotiation.

Manufacturing

- There is a need to ensure that all the required components and methods of manufacture can be accessed and are affordable.
- The manufacturing process may need to be optimized; the licensor needs to cost the optimization and review the time frames involved.

Time factors

- There is a real need to fully appreciate the time required to undertake due diligence for both the licensor and licensee entering into a negotiation. While this process must not be rushed, it is wise to set out time frames with the potential partner. These time frames may need to be built into an Evaluation or an Option Agreement.

- Ideally the licensor should draft out a licensing schedule building in time factors that relate to the patents, the out licensing process, the take-to-market route and potential income to be generated via licensing. The latter may incorporate down payments, milestone payments and ongoing royalty.

Licensing package

Access

In carrying out the due diligence the licensor will build a package of invaluable data that the potential licensee will be given stepwise access to depending on confidentiality agreements and the level of trust developed during the negotiation.

Paper trails

Licensors need to ensure that all data concerning the research that backs up the patent claims and asset package is witnessed, signed and kept in a safe place.

Show-how and know-how

There are frequently specific quirks involved in product manufacture that can't be included within the patent or very slight modifications of old processes that can't be patented but are crucial to the commercialization of a technology. These quirks may reside with specific individuals and it is essential for a licensor to access and record this show-how and know-how. We have all too often seen this type of data disappear through unexpected illness or other life changing events.

Know-how is information that resides with the licensor that will be crucial to the commercialization of the IP. It may involve drawings, market research data, customer data, trial and clinical research and much more that was not included in the patent. Know-how must be available in a transferable format.

Physical transfer

Once the licence agreement is signed the real work begins but both parties sometimes forget that it may take licensors time to really make sure that the licensee fully understands the technology or product that is being transferred. Agreements often need to incorporate time and payment for the many days or weeks that a licensor will need to spend working with the new partner to ensure smooth handover.

A few words on negotiation

Where possible try and ensure that you have access to a team able to aid the negotiation – on an as-needs basis or a virtual team; you may need to work with consultants, ensure that your patent agent can provide back up and involve your accountant and IP lawyer as part of the out licensing team. They will not need to be with you for each meeting but it's comforting to at least ensure that they will be available online if you need to break out of negotiation to ponder on a specific issue.

For negotiation meetings (home and abroad):

- Always have a written mutually agreed agenda.
- If abroad ensure that you build in rest factors to your meetings.
- Always ensure that you are aware of your expected financial package and wrap around this the lowest that you could accept and the highest that you may expect – or your starting point.

Regarding feedback and mutual agreement:

- It's a great help to the negotiation if one party can write a summary of the negotiation that took place and both parties then sign into this before moving into the next stage of negotiation.
- Keep potential licensees involved and updated with results and any changes taking place as your technology progresses and develops.

At the start of negotiations try and map out the expected deal structure incorporating any factors that may potentially cause delay.

Closing the deal is not the end to the work, it's the start of the relationship and needs to be recognized and incorporated into the deal implementation plans.

Negotiation is a skill that is in part learnt through study but is only perfected through experience. It requires clear thinking and a thorough knowledge of your product, market and potential licensee. The knowledge and confidence gained through carrying out due diligence before entering the negotiation will carry you a long way forward.

International licensing

Further information about international licensing can be found at the Britain and Ireland Licensing Executive Society (LES) website: www-les-bi.org and also at the LES international website: www.lesi.org; LES is an international organization dedicated to the enhancement of learning for those involved in the business of licensing.

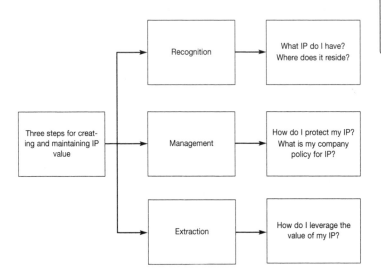

figure 1 creating and maintaining IP value

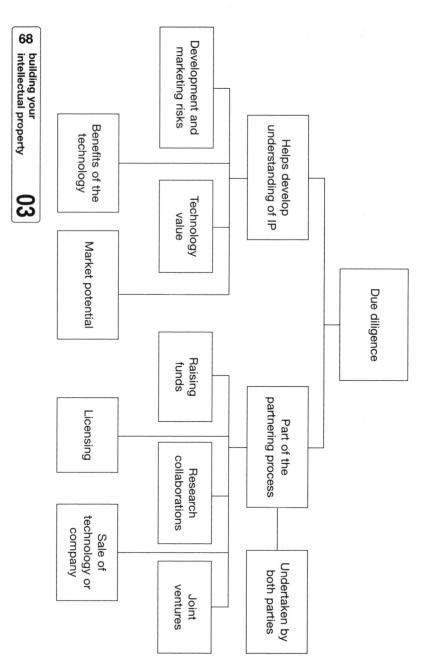

figure 2 due diligence

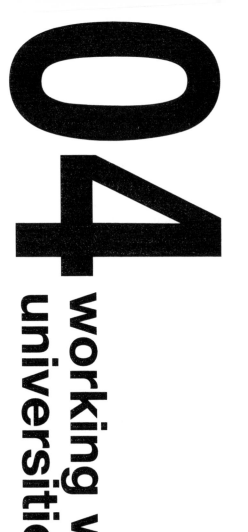

04

working with universities

In this chapter you will learn:
- how to use Lambert Model Agreement toolkits
- about making money from your ideas
- about the Fire Angel® story

4.1 Collaborative research and development

Saving time and cost when negotiating intellectual property using the Lambert Model Agreements Toolkit

Introduction

Increased business–university collaboration is essential for improved UK innovation performance. Nevertheless, the complexity and cost of negotiations relating to intellectual property (IP) can often be a serious barrier to effective collaboration between business and universities. These were some of the conclusions of the government-sponsored Lambert Review of business–university collaboration in December 2003, chaired by Richard Lambert, former editor of the *Financial Times*.

A set of model agreements, known as the Lambert Model Agreements Toolkit, was made available in February 2005 to help business and universities understand the issues involved in handling IP under a number of different collaboration situations. The Toolkit was updated in January 2006, following suggestions from users and members of the Lambert Working Group (WG) on IP who developed the Toolkit, to include further resources to help those considering collaboration. The first review by the WG of Toolkit use and uptake was conducted in February 2006 and this has been very encouraging with evidence emerging that universities, small and medium-sized enterprises, large corporates, regional development agencies (RDAs) and technology transfer training organizations are all making use of the Toolkit.

Purpose

The purpose of the Toolkit is to help businesses and universities save time and effort in the negotiation process and to increase the likelihood of a consensus between all parties. Use of the Toolkit is voluntary and the model agreements themselves are flexible enough to take account of the specific circumstances of each collaboration once both parties have agreed on which model collaboration agreement best reflects their general situation.

The Toolkit is important because the rapid pace of change in science and technology is generating new opportunities for UK business. Great strides are being made in areas such as bio- and nano-technologies, information and computer technology, new materials, and new fuels. To take advantage of this, the UK has to be able to transfer knowledge effectively, both in terms of people and know-how, between those who have generated it and those who are best placed to exploit and develop it commercially.

Solutions and applications developed by such collaborations will usually have a high intellectual input, be knowledge-intensive and provide high added-value to a business. This value is usually protected through the use of IP rights such as patents, trade marks, copyright and registered designs. Hence the model agreements are extremely important guidance tools for UK businesses and universities to ensure they get the IP right. Making it easier for such embryonic businesses to handle what is seen as a complex issue will improve their chance of survival.

Origin

The Toolkit was developed by the Lambert WG on IP, set up in May 2004 following the Lambert Review, also under the chairmanship of Richard Lambert who was determined to provide a useful and practical tool to help universities and businesses who want to collaboratively tackle this issue of complexity and cost of negotiation simply and effectively.

The WG involved over 40 different bodies with a strong interest in promoting effective business–university collaboration, including the Confederation of British Industry (CBI), the Association of University Research & Industry Links (AURIL) and the Small Business Service (SBS) as well as a number of individual companies and universities. The UK Patent Office acted as project manager to ensure the WG group completed its work on time and with the assistance of the DTI produced internet and CD-ROM based versions of the Lambert Model Agreements Toolkit which were launched in February 2005. The DTI and Patent Office act as third-party hosts for the Lambert Model Agreements Toolkit.

The Model agreements represent a compromise which strikes a balance between the interests of both parties in the collaboration.

The Toolkit elements

The Toolkit comprises a set of model collaboration agreements and a set of related resources showing how to make best use of these agreements.

The model agreements describe five different scenarios for collaborative working between business and university. These are summarized in Table 1. Three supporting tools, a Decision Guide, Guidance Notes and an Agreement Outline are also provided to help potential collaborators identify all the issues they need to take into account when trying to decide if one of the five model agreements is suitable for their particular circumstances.

table 1 the five Lambert Model Agreements (LMAs)

LMA	Terms	IP owner
1	Business has non-exclusive rights to use in specified field of technology and/or geographical territory; no sub-licences	University
2	Business may negotiate further licence to some or all university IP	University
3	Business may negotiate for an assignment of some university IP	University
4	University has right to use for non-commercial purposes	Business
5	Contract research: no publication by university without business's permission	Business

The five model agreements focus on the interaction between three key elements:

1 Ownership and freedom to use the results (usually some form of IP) from the project.
2 Financial contribution to be made by the business collaborator.
3 Freedom which the university collaborator will have over publication and communication of the results.

Using the Toolkit

Best use of the Toolkit can be achieved if a user takes a stepwise approach where:

1 They use the *Agreement Outline* to identify *all* the issues they need to consider in order to have an effective collaboration agreement.

2 They use the question and answer approach in the *Decision Guide* to decide which of the five model agreements provides the best fit with the circumstances of their collaboration; and

3 They use the *Guidance Notes* to check that they understand the meaning and relevance of all the clauses used in the model agreements.

Using this approach, it is possible to identify very quickly the important and relevant issues in any proposed collaboration, and to gain a better idea of the type of collaborative agreement best suited to the purpose in hand. Thus, when negotiations with the potential collaborator begin, the common issues can be agreed without delay and both parties can then focus their time and effort on resolving the critical issues. The model agreements serve as starting points and are designed to reduce the cost and time spent negotiating. They can be adapted to take into account the particular circumstances of each collaboration.

None of the model collaboration agreements deals with the joint ownership of IP. The Lambert WG considered that it is more difficult for the business and the university to manage this together efficiently. The Toolkit adopts a simpler approach that relies on one of the parties owning all the IP as a single entity, with the other party receiving appropriate payment and access as agreed. Also third parties seeking to license a technology will often find it easier to deal with a sole owner of all the IP.

What is important in the use of the Toolkit is to identify any major issues or differences of approach early on in the process of negotiating the collaboration agreement, so as to be able to concentrate on resolving those issues or differences. The other issues in the collaboration agreement which are essential for its effective working can be quickly agreed by both sides. The sooner agreement is achieved, the sooner the work can begin.

Other useful resources have been added to the Toolkit to help users tackle a range of related issues that often arise during collaboration projects, such as ensuring confidentiality, negotiating a licence, and use of samples provided by one collaborator to the other. These include a sample non-disclosure agreement (NDA), a sample material transfer agreement (MTA) and an example of a licence agreement. These are provided as examples only and, though consistent with the five model collaboration agreements, they were not subject to the same level of scrutiny and development.

Feedback and uptake

In February 2006, the first review of use and uptake of the Lambert Model Agreements Toolkit took place and the outcome from this has been very encouraging. The Toolkit has proven to be very useful as a practical tool to help save time and resources but also as a training tool to help those with little or no experience of negotiating collaboration agreements. The *Outline* and *Decision Guide* have proved particularly useful in this context.

Use of the Toolkit has been made across the full range of companies and universities – SMEs and large corporates such as GlaxoSmithKline (GSK) as well as well-established universities such as Oxford and Cranfield and new universities such as Hertfordshire. For example, GSK has used 31 Lambert Model Agreements for its collaborations with Universities (March 2005–January 2006), 4 of these were with universities outside the UK, and one was with a university spin-out company. All 5 types of model agreements have been used and some collaborations have been put in place at very short notice, e.g. one week.

The University of Oxford put 10 collaborations in place between October 2005 and February 2006 using Lambert Agreements – 2 with SMEs and 8 with large pharma companies. The agreements with the 2 SMEs are DTI-funded Knowledge Transfer Partnerships (KTPs, successor to the Teaching Company Scheme) and Lambert Model Agreement 4 seems particularly suited for use in this area. A number of other university users confirmed this experience – the University of Hertfordshire and Cranfield University have also found Lambert Model Agreements very useful for negotiating KTPs with SMEs.

The University of Hertfordshire has also used the Lambert Toolkit to review its policy on collaborations with industry. As a newer university with less experience in this area, they found the Toolkit to be a useful benchmark. The Model Agreements have provided useful answers on how to deal with issues on ownership of IP, confidentiality and publication of material by students. This has resulted in the successful negotiation of 8 agreements with SMEs where the Lambert input has been significant. They were also able to use the Toolkit to complete collaboration with GSK agreement in two days.

Use by universities has shown that savings of time and resources are realistic. A survey of Higher Education Institutes (HEIs) by AURIL (Association of University Research Industry Links) – (40 institutions replied) found that: the Lambert Toolkit has simplified the process of constructing contracts (72%) and saved time (61%) and resources (financial and other, 55%) during negotiations. Of those HEIs who had not used the model collaboration agreements directly, 58% said that they had used elements from the agreements in their own contracts.

Use by industry has shown that these Lambert Model Agreements can be just as effective as in-house versions but they have the added bonus of being from a third party who do not have a vested interest in the collaboration.

Business support and development bodies such as the Regional Development Agencies have also begun to use the Toolkit. The Lambert agreements have been used by the South East England Development Agency (SEEDA) as the standard agreements for its Proof of Concept Funding Scheme – PoCKeT – where local businesses are put in contact with an HEI partner anywhere from the UK to assess commercial viability (7 projects in period May 2005–February 2006; £25,000–£30,000 per project). In each of these cases a LMA type 4 or 5 (see Table 1) has been used where the industry collaborator will have ownership of the IP. SEEDA expect to have 20–30 such projects each year in this programme and that the standard agreement for the programme will be a Lambert one.

A survey by the CBI amongst its 1100 SME members received 39 responses (3.5%) highlighting the difficulty all those involved had experienced in making SME aware of the existence of this tool. Of these only 21 had experience of working with universities and only 11 had heard of the Lambert Agreements before the survey. Of these 11, 7 (64%) said the Toolkit has influenced their behaviour and 3 (27%) had used the agreements directly. Interestingly the 7 users were all SMEs with 0–249 employees. This low response rate makes drawing conclusions difficult but indicates that there is still work to be done to make SMEs aware of the existence and usefulness of the Lambert Toolkit.

Use of the DTI website www.innovation.gov.uk/lambertagreements shows that all five agreements have been downloaded in roughly equal proportion. The *Outline* has also been downloaded in similar proportion. The interactive nature of the *Decision Guide* has meant that it has received the heaviest use of all the resources on the website as users consider the effect of different combinations of factors on a collaboration. This is a good indicator that the Toolkit is being considered and used as a whole and that users appreciate the need to use the supporting materials and the agreements rather than just the agreements on their own.

Conclusion

The Lambert Model Agreements Toolkit has completed its first year in existence and the feedback from users to date is that it is achieving its objectives – it is making it easier for businesses and universities to negotiate collaboration agreements both in terms of time and cost. It is also clear that the Toolkit is valuable as a teaching tool – educating people about what is needed to have an effective collaboration agreement, what are the key issues that need to be taken into account and how they interact with each other.

All users, especially SMEs, have reported that the *Decision Guide* and *Outline* have been very helpful in improving their knowledge and identifying what they need to think about when entering into a collaboration agreement. This has led to direct use of Lambert Agreements across a wide range of collaborations and with a wide range of partners proving their usefulness and suitability. Even where Lambert Model Agreements have not be used directly, the Toolkit has been used to illustrate best practice and provide inspiration on how to resolve particular issues.

This is particularly helpful because to meet the challenges of globalization and innovation in the UK we need to increase the amount of research being done by UK businesses and the level of interaction between UK businesses of all sizes, not just the large corporates and UK universities.

A key message to get across is that the Lambert Model Agreements represent a compromise, a negotiated position between the interests of the business sponsor and the university. As such they are not the points at which a university or business might choose to start from when negotiating. Each party will get something from the agreement, e.g. in Lambert 1, Sponsor gets non-exclusive royalty-free licence to use in a specified field of technology or territory and the university owns the IP in the results. The so-called Lambert 0 approach where sponsor gets nothing is *not* consistent with the approach of the Group. The agreements represent a middle way between the interests and concerns of both sides. Lambert Agreements are *not* designed to be perfect – they are a negotiated solution and represent a compromise.

Further information

The Toolkit can be accessed directly on the DTI website at: www.innovation.gov.uk/lambertagreements. For more information about the Lambert Model Agreements and their origin, the Lambert Review and the Lambert WG on IP, and to order a free copy of the Toolkit on CD-Rom, visit: http://www.patent.gov.uk/about/ippd/knowledge/lambert.pdf.

4.2 Making money from intellectual property

This section is a case study, showing how Nick Rutter and Sam Tate made money from their intellectual property.

The FireAngel® story

All through university, Nick Rutter and Sam Tate had talked about starting their own company. Sam's expertise lay in the area of marketing and business and Nick had studied design and technology. They knew from the outset that they wanted to form a company to design, market and distribute a product. Both felt that this, rather than providing a service, would have the potential to generate better results as well as giving them greater personal satisfaction.

The business model they developed meant that their company would concentrate on design, development, branding and marketing, whilst all non-value-added functions would be sub-contracted out to experts in their specific area. Once the business model was created, all that was required was a product. After lengthy discussions and interviews with friends and family, and research with fire brigades and the Government, Nick and Sam decided to venture into the world of fire safety, and in particular, smoke alarm manufacture.

The problem

Nick and Sam identified four problems with the existing conventional design of smoke alarms:

1 Smoke and heat rises, so smoke detectors have to be situated near the top of a room or house. As conventional designs required drilling and fixing to the ceiling, a high proportion of purchasers would be put off the work involved, and the

smoke alarm would end up in a kitchen draw, still in its packaging. Also due to the positioning conventional alarms are difficult to access for maintenance.

2 The vast majority of domestic alarms are powered by a battery – research shows that almost 20% of fires fail to be detected because of missing or flat batteries in smoke alarms.

3 They are often temperamental and seen as a noisy nuisance when, for example, someone burns the toast, as again they are difficult to reset due to their position, high on a ceiling.

4 They are often viewed as ugly in our increasingly design-conscious society.

The technical solution

Nick and Sam had both completed degrees at Coventry University, and whilst studying had become aware of a graduate training programme which could provide them with the seed funding to start the project. After completion of a 12-week full-time business course they presented their business plan to a panel of expert judges to try and win the funding. They were successful, so with the beginnings of a new revolutionary product up their sleeves and with the University's support, the pioneering pair formed a spin-out company, Sprue Aegis.

In 1998 the pair filed for their first patent as the initial step to the creation of their new smoke detector. Being all too aware of the power of the brand and the need to conjure up an emblem under which they could market their product, brain storming gave rise to a new name which then became their trade mark and so FireAngel was born.

Protecting their invention

Nick and Sam were aware that they needed to protect their idea and make sure that it could not be stolen by another manufacturer before they had raised funds for development. They knew that one of the fundamental rules of IP is that they should keep their idea a secret but that this would prove difficult once they started their market research and product development in earnest.

So Nick and Sam submitted a patent specification to the Patent Office – this included drawings and a technical description of their innovation. The Patent Office then issued them with a priority date for the invention and they were then able to develop their prototype without the fear that someone else could steal their idea and claim it as their own.

Product development

Sam and Nick were faced with two choices to develop their product:

Licence their invention – they could sell the rights to use their invention to a large manufacturer who was already in the same line of business, and who could take over the development and marketing. They could negotiate a one-off fee or a share of the profits known as a royalty for this agreement which would result in a short-term profit or a combination of the two.

Go it alone – they would need to finance and research all the manufacturing processes themselves as well as making their own business contacts, but if successful the results could mean greater longer term returns.

Nick and Sam decided to stick with the courage of their convictions and go it alone. They initially received a £55,000 EU grant, but the product developed teething problems in the first year and soon swallowed this up. They raised a further £250,000 of private equity investment through a group of 'Business Angels'.

By concentrating on their core business, which was product development and marketing, and contracting out all the other elements, money was saved, and within 12 months a product certified to the relevant British Standards was available for sale in the UK. Sheer perseverance won a contract with B&Q for an exclusive sale period of three months that was followed by a two-year merchandising agreement. Other national retailers followed the lead of B&Q and within 12 months the FireAngel PS-101 Plug-In Smoke Alarm was available in over 3,000 retail outlets across the UK.

The advantages of FireAngel over conventional smoke alarms are:

- It fits between the light socket and the light bulb, so it fits in seconds, as simple as changing a light bulb.
- Turning on the light charges the integral battery. Should the battery run low, the alarm will beep once per minute, so no need for replacement batteries over the product's 10-year life.

- Silencing a false alarm is simply a matter of switching the light on and off, as opposed to climbing on chairs to push a button on the alarm, which is fixed high on the ceiling.
- As the alarm can be hidden by a lampshade, consumers find this alarm more aesthetically pleasing.

Within four years, FireAngel had won a host of awards including Real Business/CBI New Product of the Year and Sprue Aegis had developed a range of products which could be purchased in over 5,000 outlets nationwide, including major retailers, high-street stores and electrical wholesalers, as well as over the Internet.

In 2001, Sprue Aegis became a public limited company with a turnover for the quarter ended June 2003 of £515,000 – a 46% increase on the equivalent quarter in 2002. Sprue Aegis now has a workforce of 14 people. Nick and Sam have extended their IP portfolio internationally to 18 patents (either granted or in the pipeline), plus protecting a range of trade marks. A new name – AngelEye – has been registered specifically for the American smoke alarm market.

05

looking after your intellectual property

In this chapter you will learn:
- how to decide your patenting strategy
- the importance of using your trade mark correctly
- the difference between registered and unregistered designs
- how to obtain IP insurance
- about counterfeiting and piracy

5.1 Looking after your patent

If attention is paid to all stages of the patenting cycle then a strong, consistent and powerful patent portfolio can be built. Many of these aspects are looked at in other chapters in detail but it is useful to pull them together here to develop a feel for how to look after your patent.

Mining your patent

The first thing to do is to make sure that you are capturing your patents. This is sometimes termed patent 'mining' or 'harvesting' but the basic principles are simple. First of all your organization must have a central point of contact or clearing house for handling patents, coordinating the capture exercise and advertising itself as someone to come to if an employee has an idea. There are many ways to capture the ideas, by advertising internally or by organizing dedicated sessions with individuals or teams to discuss areas of work where inventions may have arisen or may arise in the future. Many organizations now have a significant reward scheme available for inventors who come forward with their ideas.

A thorough and consistent approach ensures that at least your company can consider the possibility of filing patent applications for all inventions that arise within the organization even if the eventual decision is not to proceed with patent protection.

Choosing a patenting strategy

Underlying the strategy adopted by an organization is of course the budget set aside for patenting. In the early life of a patent portfolio the principal expenses are the filing and prosecution costs which rise rapidly with the number of jurisdictions in which protection is sought. Later in the life of the portfolio an additional cost kicks in and can take over, in the form of the annual renewal fees payable to keep a granted patent alive. Whatever budget figure is arrived at it must be realistic and must take into account all aspects of the costs of patenting.

Within budget constraints the main issues to consider next are the territorial coverage of patents and whether the organization wants a focused patent portfolio or a wide-ranging portfolio sometimes termed a 'patent thicket'.

In terms of territory, in its early life a patent application can be maintained with broad potential territorial protection using the international (PCT) patent application system. This keeps the options open for two and a half years but after that the costs of individual national protection (or regional protection where available for example before the European Patent Office) become due. When deciding on territorial coverage, therefore, it is worth considering some basic points:

- Where might the invention be made? If it involves a complex or sophisticated manufacturing process then there may only be a few territories with that capability.
- Where may it be sold? If specific markets can be identified then again these should be considered.
- Where is the competition? It may well be worth targeting countries where competitors are based to make sure that you can stop infringement at source.

Against this you should ensure that some realism creeps in, not only on cost but on practicalities of enforcing patents, and in particular consider:

- Does the territory have a usable patent enforcement system? Some territories have extremely slow or unpredictable processes for enforcing patents.
- Are infringements policeable/containable? In some territories it may be very difficult to find out where infringement is taking place for example simply because of their size or remoteness. Alternatively even if an infringement is closed down it may be very difficult to stop the same entity popping up in another guise nearby and starting all over again!

When considering whether to adopt a wide or focused patenting strategy it is worth mentioning a trend that has appeared, at least in the IT sector, of patenting very broadly and aggressively. This practice is principally adopted by the big players on the basis of a 'Mutually Assured Destruction' philosophy that if one party sues another then the other party is likely to have patents to counter-sue with. In practice this is developing into a system of extensive cross licences such that in many ways patents are being used to audit new ideas and determine a modest, and worthwhile revenue from the idea. In other areas such as pharmaceuticals it is more often the case that one or a small number of patents cover a specific product providing a much more focused level of protection with much more clear space for competitors.

For the SME, budget constraints may well determine the breadth of coverage of the patent portfolio where considerations would include:

- How important is intellectual property to raising funding?
- Would a licensing strategy be beneficial? What strategy are the competition employing?

Again, after all this deliberation, the decision may be to pursue a fairly modest patent filing strategy, but at least this is a resort of a calculated decision rather than inertia.

Getting a patent granted

The investment at the outset in a well-drafted patent is worthwhile as it ensures the best prospects for effective coverage. A poorly drafted patent, whilst initially costing less, often adds far more than the initial saving later in the life of the patent application, when patent offices start raising objections to it.

During its life the patent application, before the patent is granted, may be examined by many patent offices each of whom will have a similar approach but typically with many local variations. Most territories insist that you engage a local patent attorney if you are not a national yourself and it is worth making sure that you get a good patent attorney and that you take their advice on how best to proceed, both procedurally and legally, to make sure that you obtain a strong patent as efficiently as possible.

Once the patent is granted it is worthwhile remembering that, at the administrative level, it is necessary to keep it alive by paying annual renewal fees. After a few years of regular patenting, especially if you are obtaining patents in multiple countries, these renewal fees can become a very significant part of the patent budget and so it is important to review the portfolio regularly and take a realistic view in relation to termination of granted patents which are not providing, and are not likely to provide, commercial benefit.

Enforcing patents

Finally, you want to use your patent and you also want to make sure that other people are not going to be using their patents against you.

There is little point in getting a patent unless it will make or save you money. As a result it is important to have a clear idea of what you have patented and to monitor third-party activities, especially those of your competitors, to see whether they are coming out with products or processes which you have patented. It is worthwhile remembering the power of the patent monopoly – anything that shares the underlying inventive concept covered by your patent may infringe in a territory as long as your patent is in force there. As a result the particular implementation of the concept may differ – it may be physically different – but it could still infringe. Also it does not matter whether the third party copied or had no idea of your patent. It is still enforceable.

Alternatively you may be looking for licensing opportunities. For example, your technology may be useful in implementing third-party technology to their benefit. This can provide a very welcome revenue stream but will typically involve work both in finding an opportunity and convincing the other side that the technology would merit the royalty.

It is also worth bearing in mind that the third parties may be doing the same thing with their patents. It is possible to attack other people's patents for various reasons including lack of patentability and some very powerful forms of attack are available. One of the most powerful is the European Patent Office 'Opposition' procedure whereby if a patent is successfully opposed it can be knocked out across Europe through a single, cost effective action at the European Patent Office. Any opposition, however, must be mounted within nine months of the date of grant of the European patent and so it is essential to know of any patent you might want to oppose as early as possible. This can be done easily by monitoring published patent applications which can be tracked either by technology area or by patentee, cheaply and effectively.

Generally speaking, if you are going to invest in patents you may as well look after them, and a consistent policy from capturing the ideas in the first place through to enforcing them and protecting yourself against third parties doing the same thing means you will reap the maximum benefit from your investment in the system.

5.2 Looking after your trade marks

So why is the subject of looking after trade marks important enough for a section in this book? Well, trade marks are a form of property – intellectual property, and IP is a valuable asset owned by your business. Just like real property, if you look after intellectual property well, it keeps its value better. If you do not look after it properly, things often go wrong, cost you money and you could lose your rights altogether.

Added to this, a law change is in train in the UK which moves more responsibility for looking after trade marks from the Patent Office on to the Trade Mark Owner – no more 'Nanny State'!

I have advised clients on this subject for over 20 years. It is amazing how the same themes repeat themselves. Here are some basics that are within the grasp of businesses of all sizes and are recommended as part of looking after your trade marks.

Review

Review your trade mark portfolio regularly – at least once a year. This is not just those you have already registered, but all the trade marks used in your business. This includes words, phrases, slogans, logos, etc.

Think about the products and services you sell using these trade marks. Think about the geographical markets they are used in. Are there others who use your trade mark with or without your permission?

Make a comparison between what is used in the business and what you have registered. Do they match? If there are some gaps in your registered rights think about plugging them by making more registrations. Likewise, if there are trade marks registered that are no longer used in the business you should make a note to allow the registration to lapse, or in some circumstances you may want to look at selling the trade mark on.

Make sure that in every case you use your trade marks in the correct way in order to make sure you can monopolize them. This is recommended whether or not the trade mark is registered.

Most Trade Mark Attorneys will help you with this annual review at little cost – it also helps them do their job better.

Legal requirements

You will already have some trade marks registered. Your registration will last for 10 years, and at the end of the 10-year period you will need to pay a renewal fee. Your Trade Mark Attorney will take responsibility for making sure that this renewal fee gets paid on time.

It is useful to have such a long registration period, but in 10 years a lot of water flows under the bridge. Companies move, change their names, sole traders become limited companies, businesses merge, etc. It is important to keep these kinds of details up to date on the Trade Marks Register. Your ability to pursue an infringer may be hampered if the details are out of date.

Again, if you conduct an annual review of your trade marks, your Trade Mark Attorney will recommend what actions are required at what cost, and will also be able to give you costs of renewing registrations that are coming up to the end of their 10 years. You should be able to work out an annual budget for these kind of costs as they are easy to predict.

If you do not work with a Trade Mark Attorney, you will need to have good record keeping and to keep on top of these things. It is all too easy to inadvertently allow things to lapse.

Using trade marks

There are a number of reasons why using trade marks correctly is important and will enhance your legal rights – particularly in relation to words and phrases.

What is correct use of a trade mark?

The essence of a trade mark is that it will distinguish your products or services from those of other businesses. They are a way for customers, distributors, retailers, advertisers, journalists, competitors etc. to identify your products and services or your business in general.

When you use a trade mark that consists of words and phrases it should stand out from the rest of the text, typically by capitalization at least of the leading character. It should be used as an adjective, not as a verb or noun, and wherever practicable should be followed by suitable descriptive/generic terminology.

Marking

Another useful way of identifying your trade marks is by using the ® and ™ symbols.

What is the difference? Well, the ® symbol may only be used next to those trade marks that are registered. The ™ symbol can be used next to any trade mark you 'claim' as your own, but which you may not yet have registered.

Examples of correct use of trade marks:

Clipper™ organic tea   SAMSUNG MP3 player

And examples of incorrect use:

Have a cup of Clipper   Play it on your Samsung

It is also recommended to identify yourself as the trade mark owner, for example,

'Twinings' is the registered trade mark of R. Twining and Company Limited

Why is all this important?

Rights can be lost if you use your trade mark incorrectly so that it becomes generic. There are many examples of 'lost' trade marks, e.g. Aspirin. There are also many that have survived thanks to correct use by their owners, e.g. Sellotape, Hoover.

Generic or descriptive terms are difficult to register and protect, which makes it difficult to enforce your rights.

If you have chosen a product/service/company name that is descriptive – and lots of businesses do because it helps with marketing messages – you will not be able to register it straight away and will need to build up rights through use over time. It really helps your customers etc. recognize words and phrases as trade marks if they are used along the lines outlined above.

When it comes to trying to register a descriptive word or phrase as a trade mark, having evidence of its correct use as a trade mark is a real bonus.

If you have used correctly, it is hard for infringers to argue that words or phrases, even descriptive ones, are not trade marks.

Your Trade Mark Attorney will happily review your marketing materials for you and correct any misuses of your trade marks.

Trade mark watching

I mentioned a change in UK law. This is due to happen in 2007.

As things currently stand, if you are the owner of a UK trade mark registration and somebody else applies to register a similar trade mark, the Patent Office should refuse registration and you need do nothing.

Under the change that has recently been announced, the Patent Office will no longer refuse registration, but will notify the owner of the earlier registration who can then oppose registration.

What does this mean for me?

You or your Trade Mark Attorney will start to receive notifications from the Patent Office about potentially conflicting trade mark applications. You will need to have in place a procedure for deciding whether to oppose and a diary system for making sure that the various deadlines in Opposition Proceedings are met.

Your Trade Mark Attorney will already be handling oppositions regularly and should have a system in place for dealing with the additional oppositions that are bound to arise as a result of this change in law.

There is an upside for you. When you apply to register a trade mark you will no longer encounter some of the difficult objections raised by the Patent Office where the Examiner has to imagine what the commercial realities of the market are in order to assess likelihood of confusion. In future, you may encounter an Opposition, but you will have the opportunity to negotiate a settlement without the involvement of the Patent Office's Examiner. Or the owner of the earlier trade mark may simply opt not to oppose.

The new arrangements are the same as those already in place in the EU (Community Trade Mark) system.

However, if you own a UK registration you will not be notified of a conflicting EU (CTM) application, and if you own a CTM registration you will not be notified of a conflicting UK application.

For this reason, I also recommend subscribing to a commercial watching service. This will allow you to be notified of similar trade marks being registered in specified countries or groups of countries – or world-wide if you like.

Every time you are notified, you can decide on whether the new application encroaches on to your rights.

All this will help to avoid what is known as 'dilution' of rights. Going back to the real property analogy, it is a bit like making sure nobody builds on your land, spoils your view or otherwise devalues your valuable assets – your trade marks.

Four tips for looking after your trade marks

1 Review your portfolio regularly.
2 Register and renew your trade marks.
3 Use them correctly.
4 Keep a watch on others.

5.3 Looking after your designs

One of the most common statements used, when considering how useful intellectual property (IP) rights are, is 'They are only worth what you are prepared to spend in protecting them.' Unfortunately, whilst having a grain of truth to it, the phrase does not provide the whole picture and often misleads people into not protecting their IP rights.

Designs can often be overshadowed by trade marks and patents and are sometimes regarded as the poor relative. This viewpoint and the above phrase often cause companies to overlook protection for their designs when they could be the most valuable asset of the business.

This section will explore the ways that both registered and unregistered design rights can be best utilized by the owner.

Registered designs

By registering a design the owner has formalized their ownership and rights in relation to that design. The Registered Designs Act 1949 s.7 states that the registration:

• provides the exclusive right to make, import, export, use or stock any product to which the design has been applied or is incorporated, or to let others use the design under terms agreed with the owner, in the UK and the Isle of Man;

- gives the right to take legal action against others who might be infringing the design and to claim damages. The fact that a design is registered may be enough to deter any potential infringement.

Although these rights are given to the owner when a design is registered, it is the responsibility of the owner to enforce those rights. As with other forms of property, such as land and possessions, the owner must bring any legal action against infringement in front of the courts themselves. This may appear a bleak picture which reinforces the phrase at the start of this section, but bringing an action before the courts is the last resort.

Advertising

Possibly the most simple, inexpensive and most effective method of protecting a design is to advertise that it is registered. Whenever the design is used, e.g. on packaging, the owner should clearly show that it is a registered design and state the registration number. In the majority of cases this is likely to act as a deterrent from someone infringing the design and may have the knock-on effect of them requesting a licence to use the design.

A word of warning – it is an offence under the Act to represent that a design is registered if it is not.

Notification

It is important that the owner of a design can demonstrate they have taken all reasonable steps to find a solution to a dispute before attempting to enforce the right in the courts. The owner's first step, when becoming aware of infringement, should be to notify the party concerned that they are infringing on a registered design. Using an IP attorney or solicitor to write a cease and desist letter may add weight to it and assist in dissuading any wavering infringers from continuing.

Enforcement agencies

The UK has adopted a more conjoined approach to IP crime with the Patent Office working together with trading standards, HM Customs and the police. If either trading standards or HM Customs are notified they may be able to prevent the infringer from either selling, importing or exporting their goods. In most cases this may not be possible because the infringement will be seen as a civil matter rather than a criminal one, but it is worth enquiring about.

Mediation

Disputes over the infringement and licensing of IP rights are considered suitable to be brought before the Patent Office's mediation service. The Patent Office can provide a fully accredited mediator to facilitate the proceedings or the parties can use another mediation provider. Mediation allows the parties in the dispute to explore any possible solutions without the proceedings becoming litigious and acrimonious. The benefits of this to court proceedings are:

- less expense
- agreements can be reached covering multiple jurisdictions
- there is a greater possibility of the parties being able to continue having a commercial relationship following the proceedings
- the proceedings are private and therefore commercially sensitive information will not be made open to the public

Court proceedings

Bringing a dispute before the courts should always be the last resort. It is advisable to ensure all other possible avenues of resolving the issue have been attempted. Design infringement cases are initially heard in the High Court and are normally expensive. There are several possible remedies that can be gained from court proceedings:

- injunctions
- damages
- account of profits
- destruction of the infringing articles
- delivery up of the infringing articles

It is also important that all possible attempts have been made to reach a solution prior to court action for the purpose of costs. Judges regularly increase or decrease the costs that they award depending on the efforts that have been made by the parties, and especially if a party has had an excessively litigious approach to the issue.

Groundless threats of infringement proceedings

The Registered Designs Act 1949 contains a provision for remedies against any parties issuing groundless threats of infringement proceedings. The possible remedies are:

- a declaration stating that the threats are unjustifiable
- an injunction
- damages

In light of this design owners should be careful wording any correspondence advising of possible legal action to ensure that they cannot be interpreted as a threat.

Licensing

A registered design, like any other form of property can be licensed to other parties for use under terms set out in a licensing agreement. Licensing a design can be an extremely lucrative method of fully utilizing the potential in the registration. By licensing the design the owner can gain financially from the idea without having to produce, manufacture, market, sell, etc., a product. Even if the parties have been through an infringement dispute in relation to the design there is, generally, nothing preventing them reaching a licensing agreement.

Unregistered design rights

In certain respects this right is similar to copyright in that a register does not exist for it therefore it is the owner's responsibility to prove when the design was created. Normally this is done by using a third party to witness that the design existed on a particular date, for example, paying for a solicitor to date stamp it. The owner's success in prosecuting an infringer may depend on the strength of the evidence demonstrating when the design was created.

As the right provides protection against copying it is advisable, prior to publicizing the design, to keep a record of who has had access to the design. This will assist in demonstrating how another party has had the opportunity to copy the design and therefore infringe the design right.

Owner's rights

The design right provides the owner with the exclusive right to commercially reproduce the design. As with a registered design the owner has the right to license the design for use by other parties whilst retaining the ownership. The licence must be in writing for it to be considered valid.

Infringement

Infringement of design right is divided into primary and secondary infringement.

Primary infringement occurs when a party uses the design without the permission of the right owner. The following remedies are available from an action brought before the courts:

• injunctions
• damages
• account of profits
• destruction of the infringing articles
• delivery up of the infringing articles

Secondary infringement occurs when a party:

• imports into the UK for commercial purposes
• possesses for commercial purposes
• sells, hires or offers or exposes for sale

any article which infringes a design right. If the party committing secondary infringement can demonstrate that their use was innocent they will only be liable for damages that do not exceed a reasonable royalty.

5.4 Looking after your copyright

Claiming and enforcing copyright

Copyright is automatic in the UK and most of the rest of the world. It is essentially a private right so decisions about use of a copyright work and how to enforce copyright are generally for a copyright owner to take for him or herself.

Copyright protection is automatic as soon as there is a record in any form of what has been created (there is no official registration). However, steps can be taken by the creator of a work to provide evidence that he or she had the work at a particular time. For example, a copy could be deposited with a bank or solicitor. Alternatively, a creator could send himself or herself a copy by special delivery post (which gives a clear date stamp on the envelope), leaving the envelope unopened on its return. A number of private companies operate unofficial registers, but it would be sensible to check carefully what you will be paying for before choosing this route

It is important to note, that this does not prove that a work is original or created by you. But it may be useful to be able to show that the work was in your possession at a particular date, for example where someone else claims that you have copied something of theirs that was only created at a later date.

Another useful step for a copyright owner to take when copyright material is published is to mark it with the international copyright symbol © followed by the name of the copyright owner and year of publication. This is not essential in the UK, but may assist you in infringement proceedings, and will be needed in certain foreign countries.

What about marking my work and enforcing copyright when I put it on a website?

Generally, when you put your work on a website, it is probably a good idea to mark each page of the website with the international © mark followed by the name of the copyright owner and year of publication. In addition, you could include information on your website about the extent to which you are content for others to use your copyright material without permission. Although material on a website is protected by copyright in the same way as material in other media, you should bear in mind that websites are accessible from all over the world and, if material on your website is used without your permission, you would generally need to take action for copyright infringement where this use occurs.

How can I enforce copyright?

Copyright is essentially a private right so decisions about how to enforce your rights, that is, what to do when your copyright work is used without your permission, are generally for you to take. Where your work has been used without your permission and none of the exceptions to copyright apply, your copyright is said to be infringed.

Although you are not obliged to do so, it will usually be sensible, and save time and money, to try to resolve the matter with the party you think has infringed your copyright. If you cannot do this, then you may need to go to court. Before doing so, you should consider obtaining legal advice. Courts may grant a range of remedies, such as injunctions (to stop the other person making use of the material), damages for infringement, or orders to deliver up infringing goods. If infringing copies are being imported from outside the European Economic Area, you may ask HM Revenue and Customs to stop them.

Isn't infringement of copyright a criminal offence?

Deliberate infringement of copyright may be a criminal offence. If the infringement is on a large scale (e.g. pirate or counterfeit copies of CDs are circulating) then it is worth informing the police or your local trading standards department. They can decide whether action by them, including possible prosecution, is justified.

Copyright ownership

Who owns copyright?

In the case of a literary, dramatic, musical or artistic work, the general rule is that the author, i.e. the person who created the work, is the first owner of the economic rights under copyright. This rule also applies to commissioned works. However, where such a work is made in the course of employment, the employer is the first owner of these rights, unless an agreement to the contrary has been made with the author. In some situations two or more people may be joint **authors** and/or joint **owners** of copyright.

• In the case of a film, the principal director and the film producer are joint authors and first owners of the economic rights, and similar provisions as referred to above apply where the director is employed.
• In the case of a sound recording the author and first owner of copyright is the record producer; in the case of a broadcast, the broadcaster; and in the case of a published edition, the publisher.

Copyright is, however, a form of property which, like physical property, can be bought or sold, inherited or otherwise transferred, wholly or in part. So, some or all of the economic rights may subsequently belong to someone other than the first owner. In contrast, the moral rights accorded to authors of literary, dramatic, musical and artistic works and film directors remain with the author or director or pass to his or her heirs on death.

More than one person can be the author of a copyright work

Where two or more people have created a work protected by copyright and their contributions cannot be distinguished from each other, those people are joint authors. This could apply, for example, where one person has drafted an article and another person has amended and added to it. Another example could be a broadcast made by more than one person.

Where contributions are distinct, however, each person would be the author of the part they created (if it can count as a copyright work). This could apply, for example, to a collection of poetry with each poem written by a different person.

There is a special case where the law says that two people, the producer and principal director, are joint authors of a film, unless they are the same person.

Joint authors are often also the joint first owners of copyright, but not, for example, where they have both created the copyright work in the course of employment.

Can copyright be transferred to someone else?

Copyright is a form of intellectual property and, like physical property, can be bought and sold, inherited or otherwise transferred.

A transfer of ownership may cover all or only some of the rights to which a copyright owner is entitled. But, unless a copyright owner agrees a licence for him or herself when copyright is transferred, this would mean that they would no longer be able to use the copyright work.

First or subsequent copyright owners can choose to license others to use their works whilst retaining ownership themselves.

A contractual agreement transferring ownership of copyright from one person to another is known as an assignment and is not effective unless in writing signed by or on behalf of the transferor.

Who owns copyright in a commissioned work?

When someone commissions another person or organization to create a copyright work, the first legal owner of copyright is the person or organization that created the work and not the commissioner, unless it is otherwise agreed in writing.

Even though the **legal** owner of copyright is the creator, it is possible that the commissioner may be deemed by the courts to be the beneficial owner of copyright and therefore entitled to legal ownership. This could be where the commissioner intends to stop others using or copying the work that has been commissioned, e.g. a logo design to be used as a trade mark.

Even if it might sometimes be possible for a commissioner to argue that he is the beneficial owner of copyright, it is usually helpful if copyright issues are dealt with as part of the commissioning contract so that everyone knows where they stand. In copyright law, it is possible to set out beforehand who will be the owner of copyright in a work yet to be created. It is therefore sensible for an agreement about a commission to cover ownership of this future copyright if it is desired that the owner should not be the creator. The agreement must be in writing signed by or on behalf of the creator to be effective. Commissioning contracts can also cover who is licensed to use the copyright material to be created (and what uses are possible) if anyone other than the copyright owner is to use the copyright work.

If a commissioning contract does not deal with copyright, it may still be possible for the commissioner to use the copyright work that was commissioned for a specific purpose that was understood by everyone at the time of the commission, without having to seek the permission of the copyright owner, but only for that specific purpose. (An implied licence could be argued to exist.) For any other uses, it will normally be necessary to ask the creator for permission, unless beneficial ownership is deemed to apply.

5.5 Intellectual property insurance

In 1892 Lord Esher famously remarked in the case of *Ungar v Sugg*:

> Well, then, the moment there is a patent case one can see it before the case is opened, or called in the list. How can we see it? We can see it by a pile of books as high as this [holding up the papers] invariably, one set for each Counsel, one set for each Judge, of course, and by the voluminous shorthand notes: we know 'Here is a patent case'.

> Now, what is the result of all this? Why that a man had better have his patent infringed, or have anything happen to him in this world, short of losing all his family by influenza, than have a dispute about a patent. His patent is swallowed up, and he is ruined. Whose fault is it? It is really not the fault of the law; it is the fault of the mode of conducting the law in a patent case. This is what causes all this mischief.

It is a triumph to the believers of the notion that there is no such thing as progress as that of the present day, newspapers continue to be littered with stories of legal cases where the losing party faces a legal bill in the millions.

Whilst these cases are often high profile involving the rich or notorious, and are for that reason at one end of the legal costs spectrum, the cost of litigation to your average SME remains an issue. Despite the reforms of the civil justice system implemented on the recommendation of Lord Woolf in April 1999, SMEs need to be able to muster considerable resources to comfortably fund litigation. Even with the best of cases, litigation by its very nature is risky. In England the general rule is that losing a legal action makes you liable for costs of the other side's legal team. These costs when added to your own legal costs can be significant and the resulting legal bill can be of a magnitude to threaten the stability of your company.

The rise in effectiveness and uptake of alternative dispute resolution, in particular mediation, has done much to level the playing field when SMEs face taking or defending legal actions against a much larger opponent. The fact remains however that where a case cannot be settled on a commercial basis an SME must fund a case to trial. In reality an SME is unlikely to be able to take the risky consequence of losing the action and this inevitably effects its negotiating position. A party that is unable to take matters further because of the cost of doing so is unlikely to achieve the best possible settlement.

This section is about intellectual property insurance and the role it plays in putting SMEs on an equal footing to that of much larger entities. It allows an SME the opportunity to have the financial weight behind it to enable it to protect its valuable assets against infringement and opposition.

This section also discusses 'before the event' insurance and 'after the event' insurance. It sets out the way in which insurance can be linked to a so-called conditional fee arrangement entered into with the lawyers representing an SME in an action.

In summary this section concludes that intellectual property insurance is a good thing and should be budgeted for alongside the very investment an SME makes in acquiring, maintaining and exploiting its intellectual property.

On the basis of insurance products available today, it is possible for an SME to put itself in the same position as a multinational with a significant intellectual property litigation budget. The overall effect of this is that large companies with deep pockets cannot, in the new insurance world, rely on deep pockets to remove or suppress the threat of competition from SMEs who are not infringing the intellectual property of the large corporation but who are competing fairly. Most significantly, the growth in the intellectual property insurance market should fuel the investment in intellectual property itself. Investing in, acquiring and maintaining rights becomes more attractive if there is a way in which this investment can be properly protected against infringements. Intellectual property insurance helps SMEs do just that.

Before-the-event insurance

This is the most cost effective form of insurance protection available to SMEs. It is much cheaper to buy insurance cover to fund an intellectual property action before any threat of action arises. Indeed an intellectual property insurance policy is likely to be cheaper the earlier you take it out. This means that for example in the case of patents or registered rights it should be taken out as soon as your business starts investing in those assets. If that opportunity is missed the situation should be reviewed as the business develops and the risk of infringement increases. For example, if, as an SME, you intend to license your patents, your licensee may wish you to both warrant that your intellectual property is valid and does not infringe the rights of any other person and also defend infringements that occur during the licence term. In order to be in a financial position to back any warranty and take on any infringers a business will often need insurance. Embarking on a licensing programme is therefore an event that should lead an SME into investigating and taking out insurance if it has not done so already.

It may be that as a business you already have some protection in your general or professional indemnity insurance policy. In the event of any threat to your intellectual property arising this should be checked. These general policies however will not give the level of indemnity your business will require to protect its intellectual property fully.

There are several products on the market and research should be undertaken to find the best product for your business. These products range from those that are designed to put a company in funds to conduct an investigation into intellectual property infringement to full litigation insurance. Be warned you may need around £1 million worth of cover and that means some work has to go into getting it.

Brokers tend to want to know a lot about your business before they can quote a premium especially if you wish to take out full litigation insurance. The details sought generally include details of your intellectual property and products and the business financials. The broker will also want to know about your competitors and the territories you are selling into. You will also be asked questions about whether you have ever suffered any infringement actions or, indeed have ever been threatened with any infringement actions and if so what was the outcome. Further you will generally be asked about what investigations have been made into any rights which may be held by competitors. Invariably affirmative answers to the questions about having been approached about infringement by a third party and failure to have undertaken any investigations into the intellectual property of a competitor tend to result in higher premiums.

Once the information-gathering process which can take the form of an audit of your business is complete you will be offered a policy. Premiums vary greatly depending on the type of property you have and the level of risk perceived by the underwriters.

Generally a policy will cover your business for:

- the pursuit of any claim or legal proceedings in the courts arising from an infringement or alleged infringement of your intellectual property rights
- the defence of any such claim
- the pursuit of any claim or legal proceedings arising from breach of a licence agreement or written confidentiality agreement

While you will be certain to check that the level of indemnity and premium are acceptable to cover the risk your business faces in the countries in which you trade, it is important that the detail of the policy is also checked, preferably by a lawyer. The litigation process is complex which means that only a trained litigation lawyer can really advise if the policy you are buying covers what you need it to and that you are getting value for money. For example in intellectual property matters it is often important that you have cover that allows your business to move swiftly to obtain an injunction against a company that is infringing your rights and which threatens by so doing to bring down your business. A policy which requires you to go through a process taking several weeks before it decides whether your claim is accepted may be toothless. Likewise a policy which is loosely drafted and which could allow underwriters to avoid perfectly good claims should not be agreed to.

Finally with respect to enforcement of intellectual property rights, prevention of infringement is very much better than cure. It should not be forgotten therefore that one of the major benefits of holding such a policy is the deterrent factor to would-be infringers. As such it is important that you make the fact known that you hold insurance alongside the fact that you have intellectual property rights.

After-the-event insurance

It follows that if intellectual property insurance is least expensive the earlier your business takes a policy – after-the-event insurance (ATE) is by far a more expensive option to a business who finds itself infringed and without a policy. That said, the growth in the market for ATE insurance in the last few years means that it is possible to obtain a reasonable sum to put your business in a position where it can take on significant and complex litigation at low risk to it. Policies are available to cover your own costs, the cost of the other side if you lose, and both sides' costs.

These policies, unlike before-the-event policies, are not available 'at a price' to all businesses with valuable intellectual property to protect. Policies are granted only after a rigorous assessment of the case by underwriters. In addition, ATE policies to defend an action are extremely rare. In the main polices are to fund litigation to take action against an infringer. If granted the premium is often expressed as percentage of the sum insured and are typically 20 to 30 per cent of the sum you wish to insure.

Although premiums are recoverable against your opponent if you are successful in the action, the level of premium demanded can present a business with a challenge.

By way of example, if you wish to insure against the risk of having to pay the other side's costs you need a policy that will pay out enough to cover this risk. If you are taking on a large organization you must assume that they will be likely to be represented by a large firm of commercial and specialist lawyers and that the costs bill you could face if you lose will reflect this.

A legal bill of £500,000 or more to defend a patent case cannot be ruled out. This means your premium for this type of case will be in the order of £100,000 to £150,000.

In recent times it has become possible to both borrow to fund the premium and also insure against the risk of having to pay the premium as well. In addition it is possible in many cases to spread the payment of the premium by payment in stages against agreed milestones in the litigation. In all, this means that, given time, your business could organize insurance cover that could put your business in a position to take action.

It has to be said however that even though this type of insurance is available at a cost, it does not often suit every situation. An example would be a typical intellectual property case where action must be taken swiftly such as by way of an emergency interim injunction or where an application needs to be made to the court for a search and seizure order. It is more suited to a situation where your business can survive while letting an infringer build up its business and pay you damages if found to be infringing at a full trial of the action. Where swift action is necessary before the event insurance has a clear advantage.

Insurance and conditional fee arrangements

If there is one legal phrase commonly used which says something it does not mean it is the concept of 'no win, no fee'. These words are in fact used to describe the system of conditional fee arrangements which you can enter into with your solicitor and which are a way of sharing your risk with your solicitor.

Typically they work by providing that your solicitor will be paid his costs and disbursements (which may include barristers' and experts' fees) if he wins the case perhaps with a success fee for the solicitors included. If the case is lost the solicitors' fees will not be payable. This does not mean however that your business is not liable for the disbursements incurred by your solicitor which may be significant, or the costs awarded by the court against you and payable to your opponent. In effect therefore the phrase 'no win, no fee' more accurately describes a situation of no win, no fee payable to your own solicitor.

The reason for discussing the possibility of these arrangements here is that the use and availability of conditional fee arrangements is very much linked to insurance. Conditional fee arrangements in intellectual property cases are still relatively uncommon. This is because on a practical level many solicitors are wary of entering into conditional fee arrangements for complex cases which require a significant investment of time but in respect of which it may be difficult to assess the risk of failure or success at an early stage. For example in a patent matter the case may well turn on the evidence of an expert as to whether the patent is inventive bearing in mind all the relevant prior art. A solicitor is often not in a position to say categorically whether the initial view of your intended expert is more credible than any other and therefore whether the risk is a good one.

Despite these difficulties there are some more straightforward intellectual property cases such as some copyright cases or trade mark infringement cases where the risk is easier to assess at the outset and in respect of which a solicitor may enter into a conditional fee arrangement more readily. In these cases your business will still wish to pursue the option of after the event insurance. This is because in the event that you are not successful in the action you will wish to be in a position to pay your opponents' costs as awarded against you. In these cases the fact that you have a solicitor agreeing to take your case on a conditional fee basis is a good indication (particularly if that solicitor is a specialist intellectual property lawyer) to a broker that the case has a good prospect of success and a favourable premium rate is often achievable in these circumstances.

In summary the way in which litigation is funded and conducted is changing rapidly. SMEs are increasingly in a position to secure the funding and support required to protect the investment they have made in valuable intellectual property rights.

Insurance is best secured and most cost effective when secured at an early stage and insurance premium should be budgeted alongside patent annuities and other usual business insurance products.

5.6 Enforcement of intellectual property rights

What are counterfeiting and piracy

Developing successful brands can be extremely expensive and owners invest large sums, building a business reputation that consumers recognize and support.

Counterfeiters produce fake goods and services; pirates illicitly copy others' property. Both counterfeiting and piracy can quickly destroy markets and goodwill; affecting jobs and the economy. In addition, counterfeiters have little regard for consumer safety and there is an increase in hazardous copies such as foodstuff, automotive parts and electrical goods.

Dealing with counterfeiters can be a difficult task and it is important to have some understanding of the relevant legislation to help protect intellectual property rights.

What's the relevant legislation?

Trade Marks Act 1994

The Trade Marks Act 1994 lays down criminal offences specific to counterfeiting and piracy. It protects against unauthorized copying of registered trade marks. However, trade marks need not be registered, and the Act (Section 2(2)) also seeks to protect unregistered marks through the common law right of arising out of what is known as 'passing off'.

What are the relevant legal provisions relating to counterfeiting?

Section 92 of the 1994 Trade Marks Act lays out offences concerning counterfeiting and unauthorized use of trade marks.

Trade Descriptions Act 1968

The Trade Descriptions Act 1968 came into effect on 30 November 1968. It replaced and expanded the old Merchandise Marks laws which dealt with mis-description of goods. Its particular function is to ensure, as far as possible, that people tell the truth about the goods and services they provide.

Copyright, Designs and Patents Act 1988 (CDPA)

Copyright can be complex. It legislates for the rights of authors, artists, creators and composers and for those to whom copyrights legally belong, say, by assignment. The CDPA's copyright provisions aim to prevent any unauthorized persons copying original works. Therefore it protects persons who create or own literary works; dramatic works; musical works; artistic works; sound recordings; films; broadcasts; cable programmes and so on.

There is no official system for formal registration of copyright and therefore no government register exists that lists protected works. Nevertheless, the CDPA sets out in plain language the criminal breaches and their appropriate penalties.

Copyright, etc. and Trade Marks (Offences and Enforcement) Act 2002

This Act improves enforcement tools available and brings into line the penalties, throughout the UK, for criminal copyright and trade mark offences.

In brief it removes some of the inconsistencies between the provisions applying to different IP offences and provides greater legislative transparency that should assist enforcers.

The amendments made by the Act include changes to powers of arrest in cases of offences for making illegal goods for sale or dealing in illegal goods. They improve the IP criminal offence provisions by:

- increasing maximum penalties for certain copyright and related offences, bringing them to the same level available for trade mark offences
- improving existing and introducing new police search and seizure powers in cases where illegal goods are made for sale and in cases of offences under IP law
- bringing in improved provisions for obtaining court orders for forfeiture of illegal material that may have been seized during investigation of copyright and related offences (provisions that match those that already apply to obtaining court orders in cases of trade mark offences). More information can be found at: http://www.patent.gov.uk/copy/notices/guidance.pdf

What are the criminal offences that exist for counterfeiting and piracy?

The most common ones are:

Section 92 Trade Marks Act (*unauthorized use of trade marks*)

Making or dealing in goods and packaging which bear signs identical to or likely to be mistaken for a registered trade mark; it is also an offence to possess equipment specifically designed or adapted for making these signs. The maximum penalty is 10 years' imprisonment or unlimited fines or both.

Offences under this Section of the Act are arrestable and recordable.

Section 107 Copyright, Designs and Patents Act 1988 (*criminal liability for making or dealing in infringing articles*)

Section 107 refers to the offence of dealing in articles that are believed to infringe a copyrighted work; to possess any equipment specifically adapted to making copies of copyrighted works is also an offence.

Penalties have recently been raised for more serious copyright offences involving the manufacture, importation and distribution of infringing articles (*see* The Copyright, etc. and Trade Marks (Offences and Enforcement) Act 2002). They are now in line with Trade Marks Act penalties for offences, i.e. a maximum of 10 years' imprisonment or unlimited fines or both, and all carry the power of seizure.

Section 198 Copyright, Designs and Patents Act 1988 (*criminal liability for making, dealing in or using illicit recordings*)

Section 198 relates to offences of making or dealing in recordings, which are illicit and infringe performers' and owners' rights (i.e. this is piracy or 'bootlegging'). Again, the penalties have been raised (under The Copyright, etc. and Trade Marks (Offences and Enforcement) Act 2002) bringing them into line with the Trade Marks Act, i.e. to a maximum of 10 years' imprisonment or an unlimited fine or both.

What protection does design right give?

Design right is an unregistered right and arises automatically on the first marketing of a new and novel design. It is an exclusive right for five years after first marketing and then becomes available to others subject to licences of right for the remaining five years of its term. This means that, in general, its first five years' design right is infringed when there is unauthorized trading in products to which the right is applied.

The design right owner has then the right to take civil action in the courts, seeking damages, an injunction and any other relief available for the infringement of a property right. During its final five years, anyone will be entitled to buy a licence to copy the design on their products and to sell them. However, the rights owner is not obliged to make design drawings or know-how available to licensees.

Who will help protect my IP rights?

Main enforcement agencies

In cases of counterfeiting and piracy there may be more than one offence committed and therefore there are a number of ways that the criminal law may be applied. Consequently more than one enforcement agency may become involved. The main ones are:

- the police
- Trading Standards (local government officers in England, Wales and Northern Ireland)
- Procurator Fiscal in Scotland
- HM Revenue and Customs

Police

Since counterfeiting and piracy are criminal offences the police often join with Trading Standards Officers (TSOs) and HM Revenue and Customs to develop coordinated approaches. Counterfeiting and piracy are *arrestable* offences and therefore the police have a duty to enforce the law.

In addition, Trading Standards Officers will often call for police assistance when searching premises and a breach of the peace is possible.

Trading Standards

Except in Northern Ireland where the police are the main enforcement body, TSOs have traditionally played the key role in investigation and prosecution of counterfeiting and piracy cases. Local Authorities have a statutory duty through their TSOs to enforce the Trade Descriptions Act 1968 and the anti-counterfeiting provisions in the Trade Marks Act 1994.

Section 93 of the Trade Marks Act 1994 imposes a duty on every Local Authority to enforce Section 92.

Similar provision exists for copyright offences under the Copyright, Designs and Patents Act 1988, but has not yet been brought into force.

What powers do Trading Standards Officers have? Under the Trade Descriptions Act 1968, TSOs have powers to make test purchases and to enter premises to inspect and seize goods and documents. These powers also apply under the Trade Marks Act 1994.

Where there are reasonable grounds to believe an offence has been or is about to be committed, and permission to enter the premises has been or is likely to be refused, TSOs can apply to a Justice of the Peace for a warrant to search.

HM Revenue and Customs

The Trade Marks Act 1938 introduced a system of notification which allows trade mark owners to notify HM Revenue and Customs (HMRC) of potential infringing goods being imported into the country. This system continues under Section 89 of the 1994 Trade Marks Act. Similar provisions exist for other types of IPR infringement in the Copyright, Designs and Patent Act 1988. More information can be found at: http://www.hmrc. gov.uk/forms/forms/c1340.pdf

HM Revenue and Customs and related EC regulations

European Community (EC) regulations work alongside UK provisions to establish barriers to the importation of counterfeit and pirated goods across the external borders of the EC. This brings EC legislation into line with the internationally agreed provisions of the Trade-Related Aspects of Intellectual Property Rights (TRIPs Agreement).

Where a notification is made and goods fitting the description are found. HMRC will either suspend release of the goods or detain them. HMRC must then inform the parties involved that they have been intercepted. Usually they will also send a sample of the goods to the brand owner for inspection.

If HMRC are satisfied the goods are illicit they will seize the items and give warning to the owner who is entitled to contest the action. Where goods are found to be liable for forfeit, the goods will be destroyed or disposed of outside normal commercial routes. Compensation is not an option.

Can traders justify the sale of counterfeit goods by using disclaimers?

Disclaimers that state 'these goods are counterfeit, 'these goods are fakes' or 'brand copies' do not assist as a defence, under the Trade Marks Act. In fact it is an admission that the goods are illicit.

What if a trader unwittingly offers counterfeit or pirated goods for sale?

It is a defence under Section 92 of the Trade Marks Act 1994 to show that he/she believed on reasonable grounds that the use of the trade mark was not an infringement of its owners' rights. However there may still be a case to answer under civil law.

Where can I find provisions relating to civil proceedings?

Sections 14–21 in the Trade Marks Act 1994.

How else are brand owners able to protect their rights?

Many brand owners have their own anti-piracy teams and for these tackling counterfeiting and piracy can involve bringing a combination of civil and criminal actions. You can contact the following organizations for advice on counterfeiting and piracy matters (others appear on the Patent Office web page: http://www.patent.gov.uk/about/enforcement/index.htm).

Alliance Against Counterfeiting & Piracy (AACP): http://www.aacp.org.uk/

Anti-Copying in Design (ACID) http://www.acid.uk.com/

Anti-Counterfeiting Group (ACG): http://www.a-cg.com/

British Music Rights: http://www.bmr.org/

British Phonographic Industry (BPI): http://www.bpi.co.uk/

British Video Association: http://www.bva.org.uk/

Business Software Alliance (BSA): http://www.bva.org.uk/

Crimestoppers: Freephone 0800 555 111

The Entertainment and Leisure Software Publishers Association (ELSPA): http://www.elspa.com/

Federation Against Copyright Theft (FACT): http://www.fact-uk.org.uk/

Federation Against Software Theft (FAST): http://www.fast.org.uk/

HM Revenue and Customs: http://www.hmrc.gov.uk/business/index.htm

IFPI: http://www.ifpi.org/

International Chamber of Commerce (ICC) Counterfeiting Intelligence Bureau (CIB): http://www.iccwbo.org/ccs/menu_cib_bureau.asp

Local Authorities Coordinators of Regulatory Services (LACORS): http://www.lacors.com/pages/trade/lacors.asp

Mechanical-Copyright Protection Society (MCPS): http://www.mcps.co.uk/

REACT Services (UK) Limited E-mail: twilliams@react.uk.net

5.7 Companies and the law[1]

This section provides an overview of the protection of the company name, an aspect of IP which is directly relevant to the registration of companies.

Company names, business names and trade marks

Setting up the company – choice of name

When setting up a company, it is obviously necessary to decide on the name of the company. Once decided upon, it is important to do an initial search of the Index of Company Names which is maintained by the registrar of companies. This search can be done easily (and at no cost) via the Companies House website: http://www.companieshouse.gov.uk.

The purpose of this initial search is to make sure that there is not an existing company with the same name. For reasons discussed below, when conducting this initial search, it is also useful to consider whether, even if the chosen name is not the same as an existing company, the name is not 'too like' the name of an existing company.

If, on subsequently making an application for registration of the company, the registrar considers that the name of the company is the same as that of an existing company, the application for registration of the company will be refused. Given this possibility, it is important not to expend any money (for example, on stationery) on the assumption of securing that name.

---

[1] This section first appeared in *Register* magazine (MMIV)

Even if registration of the company (Newco) with the chosen name is secured, other problems may still arise. There are a number of possible scenarios to bear in mind.

Name is 'too like' the name of an existing company

Following the registration of Newco, an existing registered company may object to the registration on the ground that the chosen name is 'too like' the name of the existing company, hence the suggestion above that this possibility be borne in mind when making that initial search of the Index of Company Names.

In deciding whether the name is 'too like' an existing name, the registrar will look at the two corporate names and only if they appear to be like each other, does he or she consider whether they are 'too like', that is, if there is a danger of confusion between companies.

Where the objection is upheld (Newco will be given an opportunity to put forward evidence to justify retaining the name), the registrar will make a direction that Newco change its name. This may prove an expensive exercise depending on the consequential changes which this will involve, for example, to stationery and signage.

A glance at the relevant statistics for a three-year period (see Table 2) shows that this possibility of a direction to Newco to change its name is a risk that companies need to be aware of, though a direction of this nature may only be made within 12 months of the date of registration of Newco.

table 2 Statistics for a three-year period

Years	Objections received by the registrar	Directions made
2001/02	655	262
2002/03	638	231
2003/04	792	278

The other side of the coin is that, once Newco is registered, the directors should check from time to time on the Index of Company Names to ensure that other businesses have not registered a company name which Newco would wish to object to on precisely these grounds – that it is 'too like' the name of Newco.

A conflict with an existing business name

Assuming that the chosen name is safe from challenge under the Companies Act 1985, there remains the possibility that its use will be challenged by a business which has been using this name as a trading name but which has not registered it as a trade mark. Business or trading names are regulated by the Business Names Act 1985 but there is no requirement for them to be registered.

In this scenario, the competitor business may decide to protect its goodwill in the name by bringing an action against Newco for passing off. A passing off action can be brought where:

- the claimant can establish that there is *reputation* or goodwill attached to his goods or services which are known by some distinctive feature – in this case the trading name
- there is a *misrepresentation* by the defendant (through its choice of name), whether or not intentional, leading or likely to lead the public to believe that the goods or services offered by the defendant are the goods or services of the claimant
- that the claimant has suffered or is likely to suffer *damage* as a result of the erroneous belief engendered by the defendant's misrepresentation (*Reckitt & Colmon Products Ltd v Borden Inc* [1990] 1 All ER 873 at 880).

The risk of attack on these grounds may be slight as establishing each of these elements can be difficult and passing off proceedings are costly to bring; but it cannot be ignored. For example, Blackburn Local Authority brought a successful passing off action against a company which had incorporated in 2002 with the name 'Blackburn Transport Ltd'. The local authority had from 1986 operated its bus services under the name 'Blackburn Transport' and the defendant company was competing aggressively with the local authority's services.

Again, for the future, the directors of Newco should be vigilant for businesses trading under a business name which would give grounds for a passing off action by Newco.

A conflict with a registered trade mark

Another possibility which must be considered is that the chosen name of Newco infringes a registered trade mark or a mark for which an application for registration has been made. Registration by Companies House is not a guarantee that there is no infringement of a trade mark and the registrar of companies does not consult the Trade Marks Register when considering an application for registration of a company.

Infringement of a registered trade mark is a serious matter which will almost certainly result in immediate request to Newco to change the company name. If the directors are unwilling to change the name, infringement proceedings are the likely outcome which can result in orders requiring the company to change its name and, possibly, also the award of damages.

For example, the Halifax, the well-known high-street provider of financial services, brought a successful action for trade mark infringement and passing off against companies incorporated as 'Halifax Repossessions Ltd', 'Halifax Second Mortgages Ltd' and 'Halifax Business Finance Ltd'. Likewise, IBM, the computer giant, brought an action against a company which changed its name to Web-Sphere Ltd. IBM is the registered proprietor of the WEBSPHERE trade mark for computer software etc.

Therefore, to guard against these problem and prior to the formation of Newco, a check should be made against the register of trade marks to make sure that no one has registered the chosen name as a trade mark.

The register of trade marks is maintained by the Patent Office and can be inspected on line at http://www.patent.gov.uk/tm/dbase/index.htm. While it is possible to carry out a search directly, searching is a skilled task and it may be advisable, though more costly, to have a full trade mark search conducted by a trade mark attorney. Another option is to use the Patent Office Trade Marks Search and Advisory Service which is discussed in more detail below. Searching will reveal any potential difficulties before Newco finds itself in the position of having infringed another business's intellectual property rights. The choice of method of searching will depend on the scale and nature of the new business and the resources of its promoters.

Registering the company name as a trade mark

It may be that Newco itself should consider registering the company name as a trade mark where the name is distinctive and distinguishes the business from other businesses. Without a registered trade mark, Newco can only protect its unregistered trading name by a passing off action which, as noted above, are difficult to win and expensive to bring.

The advantage of registering the company name as a trade mark is that the company is then the proprietor of a registered trade mark. The proprietor has exclusive rights in the trade mark which are infringed essentially by:

- the use of an identical trade mark in the UK without his consent in respect of identical goods or services; or
- the use of a similar trade mark with respect to goods or services which are the same as (or similar to) the goods and services for which the mark is registered where there is a likelihood of confusing the public.

Available remedies in cases of infringement could include an injunction restraining the future conduct of the infringer and/or damages, subject to some limited defences. However, infringement proceedings may not be necessary as a letter pointing out the existence of the registered trade mark is often sufficient to bring the problem to an end.

To secure these advantages, the company name must be acceptable for registration as a trade mark. Trade marks are regulated by the Trade Marks Act 1994, as amended, and registered with the Patent Office. For a mark to be registered, it must:

- be distinctive for the goods or services it will apply to
- not be deceptive, immoral or against the law
- not be identical or similar to any earlier marks for the same or similar goods or services.

Even if the directors think the chosen name meets these criteria, further professional advice is advisable, given the complexities in this area of law.

In this context, the Patent Office itself provides a valuable service whereby anyone thinking of applying for registration can ask for advice as to whether the mark meets the requirements for registration and whether it conflicts with an existing mark. This Trade Marks Search and Advisory Service (cost £80 plus VAT for each trade mark, at the time of writing) can save applicants from the expense of making an application for registration which has little or no chance of being accepted for registration. It is useful to have assistance at this preliminary stage because once an application for registration has been made for a trade mark, it cannot be altered and the Patent Office cannot refund the application fee (currently £200 for one class of goods or services plus £50 for each extra class of goods or services for which registration is sought). As noted above, use of this service ahead of forming Newco will also avoid problems with incorporating a company with a name which infringes an existing trade mark.

The fact that the preliminary advice from the Advisory Services is that the application is acceptable is a definite opinion that the mark is distinctive. However, it is not a guarantee of registration for the application for registration must be advertised and other businesses may object to its registration. A period of three months has to be allowed for this purpose. It follows that the process of registration of a trade mark does take several months. The Patent Office aims to register 90 per cent of applications, where no substantive objections have been raised, within eight months of the application.

Given the timescales involved, once Newco has been registered at Companies House and the company name secured (subject to the possibility of challenge on the 'too like' basis), an application for registration of the company name as a trade mark should be made (assuming it meets the criteria for registration). Hence, it is sensible to use the Trade Mark Search and Advisory Service at an early stage so that once registration of Newco is secured, the application for registration of the name as a trade mark is ready to be submitted.

Domain names

Finally, some general points about domain names. A domain name is the name by which the company is known on the Internet. It is not the case that registering the domain name will ensure that Newco can register the same name as a trade mark: it may not meet the criteria for trade mark registration. Likewise, registering a name as a trade mark does not entitle Newco to the same domain name.

It should also be noted that registering a name as a domain name may in itself amount to passing off, as the Court of Appeal accepted in *British Telecommunications plc v One in a Million Ltd* [1988] 4 All ER 476. The court there could conclude that use of a domain name which would, by reason of its similarity to an existing company name or registered trade mark, inherently leading to passing off could be restrained by injunction. The defendants, who were dealers in domain names, had registered domain names comprising the company names or registered trade marks of the plaintiffs.

This approach is similar to the approach which the courts had already taken with respect to so-called '*opportunistic incorporations*', as illustrated in *Glaxo plc v Glaxowellcome Ltd* [1996] FSR 388. In that case, in anticipation of a merger of Glaxo and Wellcome, the defendants incorporated a company with Glaxowellcome, the two pharmaceutical companies having indicated that the name of the merged company would be Glaxo-Wellcome. The defendants were willing to sell the company to Glaxo for £100,000. Lightman J rejected

> any such pre-emptive strike of registering companies with names where others have the goodwill in those names, and the registering party then demanding a price for changing the names. It is an abuse of the system of registration of companies' names. The right to choose the name with which a company is registered is not given for that purpose (at 391).

A mandatory injunction was granted requiring the defendants to change the name of the company. Lightman J agreed that a party prejudiced by this type of conduct is not obliged to wait for the registrar of companies to issue a direction for a change of names, as discussed above, but can proceed with an action for passing off.

Useful websites

Companies House: http://www.companieshouse.gov.uk

See also Companies House Guidance Booklets on Companies Names and Business Names which are available on the website.

UK Patent Office: http://www.patent.gov.uk

Nominet UK is the registry for .uk Internet names and it manages the authority database of .uk domain name registrations. For more information on registration of domain names, see http://www.nominet.org.uk/index.html.

For information generally on intellectual property, see http://www.intellectual-property.gov.uk.

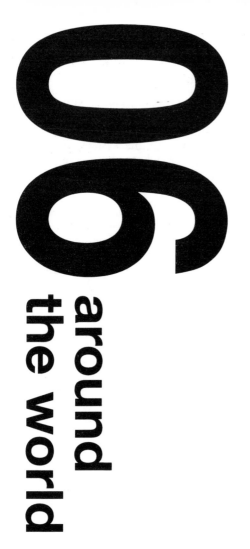

06

**around
the world**

In this chapter you will learn:
- how to protect patents in Europe
- about international patent filing
- about community trade marks and designs
- how to protect trade marks worldwide

6.1 European patent protection

The European Patent Office (EPO) was established almost thirty years ago as a direct result of an inter-governmental treaty – the 1973 European Patent Convention (EPC). It provides an alternative route to acquiring national patent protection in numerous European countries through a centralized procedure, and as such those countries which have joined the European Patent Organisation have effected a delegation of their sovereign powers to grant patents valid in their territory to the EPO. Consequently, whilst the UK Patent Office might grant around 10,000 patents per year, the EPO grants over five times as many patents per year which are binding in the UK. The EPC is not European Community legislation, and the EPO is not a body of the European Commission, although all the current member states of the European Union are also members of the European Patent Organisation.

Patent protection through the European route is for the most part the same as that described through the national route (*see* Section 1.2). Therefore, this section will focus on its differences, rather than its similarities with the national systems. Particularly it should be noted that the (current) 31 members[1] of the EPC have amended their national patent laws to be aligned with the provisions of the EPC, so that both the EPO and the national patent offices all apply the same basic criteria when considering questions of patentability. Issues of novelty and inventive step, as well as excluded subject matter (e.g. discoveries or mathematical theories) are now uniform across all EPC contracting states. Of course, national courts are still the forum for patent disputes, and the case law from those courts can diverge from one country to the next. Each country has its own body of case law, and its own legal traditions, whether common law (e.g. UK) or civil law (e.g. France).

Applications are processed in English, French or German (the three 'official languages' of the EPO). Applications from US or Japanese companies are typically filed in English, as are those from European companies which are having to prepare English translations to file in the US. Consequently about 70 per cent of applications coming to the EPO are in English.

---

[1] For a full list of EPC contracting states, please see http://www.european-patent-office.org/epo/members.htm

An application might claim priority from earlier applications first filed at national patent offices within the 12-month priority period. (The earlier applications might also have been searched at the national patent offices too, without prejudice to the search which the EPO will perform.) Alternatively an application might enter the EPO via the PCT route (see Section 6.2), because an applicant for an international patent application has designated the EPO as a region for patent protection.

An application consists of:

- a complete description and drawings (if necessary)
- one or more claims (on which a search will be performed)
- an abstract summarizing the invention for inclusion in, e.g., patent information databases
- information identifying the inventor(s) and applicant(s)
- designation of at least one contracting state later. [2]

As with the national systems, publication then follows, typically 18 months after the priority date. The publication serial number will have the suffix 'A1' if it is published with its search report, or with the suffix 'A2' if the search report was not ready at the time of publication. When the search report is ready at a later date it will be published under the same serial number, but with the suffix 'A3'.

Publication of the application discloses the invention to the world. This means that rivals will now know what you are up to, but potential partners will also be aware of your latest technological activity, and may wish to discuss a deal.

[2] On filing all contracting states are designated automatically by means of a pre-crossed box on the application form (downloadable from the Internet). After receipt of the search report, the applicant must pay a designation fee for each contracting state where he or she desires to maintain protection. Whilst this does not oblige the applicant to pay for grant in those countries at a later date if he or she chooses not to take up protection in those countries, it is worth remembering that an applicant cannot later designate a state that was not on his or her list originally. The actual states in which the patent will be effective are determined post-grant (e.g. by not filing translations or otherwise fulfilling formalities requirements required to enjoy protection in certain contracting states).

No other person may now file a patent application for the same invention which would succeed, because their application will lack novelty in view of your disclosure – and this is true whether or not your own application is later granted. Furthermore, if your rivals begin to copy your invention you will be able to sue them for damages, once your patent is granted, with respect to any infringing activity after your publication date. After all, this is the date on which you put the world on notice: 'Watch out! Patent pending!'

Then follows the examination procedure. The examiner will use the citations found during the search stage, and if necessary will object to parts of the claims and/or description. The applicant's attorney will respond according to his or her client's wishes and an exchange of correspondence will be entered into. There is no limit to the amount of such exchanges and each response from the examiner comes with a time limit for response by the applicant (per his or her attorney). Some time limits may be extended, subject to the payment of a surcharge. In the UK, extensions to such time limits are given at no cost, but only for a good reason. However, the UK operates a statutory guillotine period of four and a half years[3] from the priority date by which time the application must be granted or it is terminated. At the EPO no such guillotine exists.

When the examiner and the applicant (via their attorney) have agreed the final form of the claims, and resolved any other matters, the application is ready to be granted. At this stage translation of the granted claims into the other two official EPO languages must also be provided. The patent is then published under its original serial number, but with the suffix 'B1' – which denotes it is the granted form of the patent.

Opposition

Once published in granted form, the patent application becomes open to 'Opposition' by third parties, typically commercial rivals, who believe that one or more of the claims should not be granted for any of a variety of reasons. Such rivals have a window of just nine months from the publication of the mention of the grant in which to file their opposition with evidence and reasoned arguments.

[3] This is the so-called 'Rule 34' period. It may be longer for those applications on which a first examination report was not issued within $3^{1}/_{2}$ years of the priority date. It is extendable only under limited prescribed circumstances.

The grounds for opposition are restricted, but include: lack of novelty; lack of inventive step; the claims relate to excluded subject matter (e.g. a mere discovery); insufficient disclosure; and added subject matter. Opposition is an administrative process, and is subject to appeal before the EPO Boards of Appeal. If you oppose a rival's patent and win, then you will have knocked out their rights across all of Europe with a single action. Trying to attack a rival's patent at a later stage can be far more costly, as it would need to be carried out in a multitude of national courts.

Legal decisions coming down from the Boards of Appeal form part of the body of patent case law in Europe, and can be considered by national courts when reaching decisions on local patent disputes. This helps to harmonize the interpretation and application of patent law across the diverse national courts. There are about 3,000 oppositions filed every year (i.e. about 5 per cent of all granted European patents are opposed), and about 2,000 decisions issued.

Translations

Once a European patent has been granted its unitary form ends and the patentee is left with a bundle of national rights, subject to their respective national patent law. However, for these national patents to come into effect they must be validated in each contracting state where the patentee wishes to enjoy protection. This means that certified translations into the languages of the particular contracting states must be filed with the national patent offices in question, often along with the payment of a fee and publication of the translated patent. So whilst you might have designated Spain on your application, and achieved a granted patent, you will have no enforceable rights in Spain until a Spanish translation of your granted patent is lodged with their patent office, the relevant fees are paid and the translation is published in the *Spanish Patent Gazette*.

The Community patent

We already have unified trade mark and design registration systems for the European Community (since 1994 and 2002 respectively), and calls for a unitary patent system applying across the whole Community have been strong for many years. The member states have agreed to provide a centralized patent granting procedure for Europe, successfully concluding the EPC in 1973. The outstanding contentious issues from that time however, regarding the regime to create and enforce a unitary

Community-wide patent right, were packaged into the Community Patent Convention (CPC).

It is over 25 years since the then nine members of the European Community signed the CPC. Because certain details were unresolved it was not ratified by national governments, and hence has not come into force, yet it has had a considerable harmonizing influence on European patent law as all the EPC contracting states have aligned their national substantive patent law along the lines of the provisions of the CPC.

At the core of the issue is the cost of patent protection in Europe, when compared with e.g., the USA. The application fees[4] at the EPO typically amount to over €4,000, and attorney costs can double or triple that bill. Estimates vary, but what is not in doubt is that patent protection for the same invention in, e.g., the eight largest EU markets will cost on average five times as much as protection in the USA, where the single market represents 360 million persons.[5] Whilst the EPO provides a centralized single granting procedure, and is a huge step forward when compared with individual national filings in EU member states, what follows post-grant imposes a burden on industry which is unique to Europe.

Firstly, there is a requirement to file translations of the full patent at the national patent offices of every country in which protection is to be enjoyed. So, if you started in English, paying for translations into French, German, Italian and Spanish would get you protection in up to 10 EPC contracting states. You would need many more translations to enjoy protection in all 31 EPC contracting states.

Secondly, granted European patent rights become individual national rights, to be licensed and litigated independently in national courts. This means that your rights in one country could be struck out by a local court action, but maintained in others. It also means that your rights need to be renewed annually in each contracting state according to the local tariff. (Half of this income goes to the EPO, who did the search, examination and grant, and half stays with the national patent office, who maintain registers and perform other administrative duties.)

---

[4] For up-to-date information on fees at the EPO please see http://www.european-patent-office.org/epo/fees1.htm
[5] Whilst acquiring patent protection in the US is, on average, cheaper than in Europe, it is worth remembering that patent enforcement and litigation in the US is, on average, more expensive than in Europe.

Consequently, industry has lobbied for a single EU-wide patent right, enforceable equally and consistently across all member states in a single language and which can be licensed, litigated and renewed as a single entity.

These language and jurisdictional issues were precisely the points on which agreement was elusive over 30 years ago when the European patent system was first being created. Although negotiations on the Community patent are currently stalled, the outstanding issues remain: (i) how to set up a court which can adjudicate on questions regarding a Community-wide patent right; and (ii) which language regime should prevail. Naturally, a single language would be the cheapest solution, but difficult to achieve politically; and should a Community patent come to pass imposing a substantial translation burden on applicants it would not provide the economic benefits over the current system for which industry is calling.

In the absence of a successful resolution of the Community patent at this time, the member states have put their energy into parallel alternative solutions to these two issues, both of which are hoped to bear fruit soon.

i) The European Patent Litigation Agreement (EPLA)[6]

Negotiations between contracting states have been continuing for six years to establish a central European Patent Court to hear patent infringement and revocation actions. According to the latest draft proposal such a court of first instance would have a central division and regional divisions (i.e. be located in several places across Europe) and would have a Court of Appeal.

Ideally the court should be able to finance itself through fees charged to litigants, but if this makes the forum too expensive then it may be subsidized by the contracting states. The procedural provisions should be much like any regular civil or common law court (e.g. with regard to case management, submission of evidence, publicity, 'loser pays costs', etc.); and the court would enforce the usual sanctions (e.g. damages, injunctions, freezing orders, etc.). A successful revocation action would knock out the patent in all EU states in a single blow. Cases would be heard by panels of three or five judges, comprising a mixture of legal and technical expertise. Hearings would be conducted in English, French or German.

---

[6] For more information see http://patlaw-reform.european-patent-office.org/epla/index.en.php

ii) The London Agreement[7]

In an attempt to reduce the burden of translation costs on applicants with granted European patents the London Agreement was concluded in October 2000. This agreement would require the contracting states to waive, entirely or largely, the requirement for translations of European patents to be filed in their national language. When the patent is validated in a contracting state sharing an official language with the EPO the applicant would no longer have to file a translation of the patent specification. Where this is not the case, the applicant would be required to submit a full translation of the specification only if the patent is not available in the EPO language designated by the country concerned.

This agreement is subject to ratification in a quorum of contracting states before it can come into effect. Sadly, the ratification conditions have not quite been met at the time of writing. It is hoped that this agreement will come into effect in the near future, and industry can begin to save some money on translations for its granted patents.

6.2 International patent protection: strategic issues for SMEs

For small and medium-sized enterprises (SMEs), patenting an invention in many jurisdictions can provide a competitive advantage in export markets but also requires careful planning. If care is not taken to identify the most appropriate strategy, the rapid spiraling of costs could be crippling. The Patent Cooperation Treaty (PCT) is a tool that may be used to overcome some of the main barriers SMEs face when patenting abroad. It provides the opportunity for filing a single international application with effect in over 125 countries, delaying costs and providing valuable time and information for SMEs to take informed decisions on whether and in which countries to continue the application process.

---

[7] For more information please see: http://patlaw-reform.european-patent-office.org/london_agreement/index.en.php

There may be many reasons why an SME may decide that patenting abroad is a good idea. These may include one or more of the following: (1) the company wants to expand into new markets with innovative products and would not be able to compete with companies that have not incurred the same research and development (R&D) costs; (2) the company already operates in various markets and wishes to introduce the innovative product in the markets in which it has an established presence; (3) the commercial viability of the invention may require the company to exploit the product beyond its national boundaries and benefiting from exclusive rights is considered crucial; (4) the company may wish to license the invention out to companies in foreign markets which it would not be able to serve on its own; (5) the patented invention may be a platform technology that could be licensed out to several companies in various markets in exchange for royalties. Other reasons might include patenting abroad to outsource production of the innovative product to another country, or to enter into cross-licensing agreements with foreign companies, or to attract foreign investors.

Whichever the reasons are, SMEs seeking to patent their inventions internationally are often faced with a key concern: how to control the costs of filing applications in multiple jurisdictions, particularly in the early stages, before the inventions have even been commercialized. The costs of filing patent applications would generally include those relating to the official filing fees in various jurisdictions, the translation of the applications into the relevant national language and the hiring of national attorneys who will represent the applicant before the patent office. Such costs would generally be incurred within 12 months from the date in which they have filed their first application in their own country.[8] For a company that is yet to understand whether the patent is likely to be granted, that is not sure whether the invention will prove successful in the marketplace, or is yet to find a licensee or investor who is willing to partner to take the product to market, all such costs could be an insurmountable hurdle.

---

[8] Twelve months is the duration of the priority period, as provided for by the Paris Convention on the Protection of Industrial Property.

The applicant will have to weigh this against the knowledge that without patent protection in foreign jurisdictions, it will not benefit from exclusive rights in those markets. Patents, in fact, are territorial rights, which means that inventions are only protected in countries (or regions) for which a patent application has been applied for and has been granted. In countries for which no patent application for a given invention has been filed, the invention will be considered to be in the public domain and it would be very difficult to stop free riders from commercializing products embodying the invention, or to license the invention to other companies in exchange for royalties. How can this fundamental hurdle be overcome?

Using the PCT

The PCT[9] is used by companies in over 125 countries as a means to overcome this major hurdle, providing applicants with **18 additional months** (on top of the 12-month priority period) during which they can explore the commercial potential of their product in various countries and decide where to seek patent protection. During that period they will also benefit from an international search report and an opinion on patentability, which will give applicants a good indication as to the likelihood that their applications will meet the patentability requirements and will proceed to grant. With this information in hand, applicants can assess the situation, amend the patent claims if necessary and take an informed decision on whether to continue with the application process and if so, in which countries.

The payment of the national filing fees, translation costs and national attorney costs are, therefore, delayed and costs of filing in countries in which the applicant is no longer interested in are saved altogether. This makes the system very appealing to SMEs who will be particularly concerned about costs throughout the application process.

The use of the PCT has experienced enormous growth in recent years. In 2005, 134,000 PCT applications were filed, representing a 9.4 per cent increase over the previous year.[10]

[9] More information on the PCT available at: http://www.wipo.int/pct/en/
[10] WIPO press release 436. For further statistics on the PCT, see: http://www.wipo.int/ipstats/en/statistics/patents/

Filing an international application

In order to file an international application under the PCT, applicants need to have a direct link, either by nationality or residence, with a country that is a member of the PCT, as is the case of the UK. Companies that have an establishment in the UK, therefore, can benefit from the system and apply for protection in over 125 countries through a single application. This application may be filed at the UK Patent Office or directly at the International Bureau of WIPO in Geneva, Switzerland. Either way, a single PCT application is filed, in one language and with one set of fees, having legal effect in all PCT member countries. This effect significantly reduces the initial transaction costs of submitting separate applications to each patent office.[11]

An important point for applicants is that a PCT application may claim priority from earlier applications. What this means is that a company that files a patent application in one country can file a PCT application for that same invention during the 12-month priority period. Typically, companies based in the UK would file a national application at the UK patent office and file an international application just before the expiry of the priority period, thus benefiting from the additional 18 months provided by the PCT to take decisions as to where to prosecute the patent. The international application is then examined to ensure that it meets a series of formal requirements.

International applications are increasingly filed electronically using the PCT-SAFE and PCT-EASY systems. In 2005, for the first time, the number of applications filed on electronic media exceeded paper filings.[12]

[11] Guidance on how to submit an international application under the PCT can be obtained from national patent offices and at www.wipo.int/pct

[12] Information on electronic filings under the PCT are available at: http://www.wipo.int/pct-safe/en/

The international search report, examination and opinion on patentability

Once an application has been filed and checked to see whether it meets formal requirements, it is sent to one of the International Searching Authorities (ISA) which will search the prior art to reveal documents disclosed prior to the international filing date. On the basis of the prior art revealed during the search, the ISA will issue an international search report and a 'written opinion' on patentability.

At this stage, the applicant cannot intervene in the process or present arguments before the ISA. However, the information provided by the ISA will be crucial for strategic decision-making. Depending on the prior art documents revealed in the report and the opinion on patentability, the company may decide to continue with the application process if the prospects are looking good, demand a 'Chapter II' examination from an International Preliminary Examining Authority during which it will be allowed to intervene and present arguments, make amendments to the claims, or withdraw the application altogether.

Publication

The international applications are published by the International Bureau of WIPO, together with the international search report, after the expiration of 18 months from the priority date, unless they are withdrawn before technical preparations for publication are complete (usually $17\,^{1}/_{2}$ months from the priority date). At that point in time the international application becomes part of the prior art. This is important because patent offices around the world when examining other patent applications and deciding on their patentability will take the published PCT application into consideration as part of the prior art.

The applicant may request earlier publication if he or she wishes, but an additional fee is payable if the international search report has not yet been established, since it will then be necessary to republish the application when the report becomes available.

The national phase

At 30 months from the priority date, once the search and examination has taken place and the application has been published, the so-called 'international phase' of the PCT is completed and the application enters the national phase. This is the point in which applicants will have to present national translations of the applications to the national (or regional) patent offices and pay the applicable national fees. The use of the PCT has, therefore, delayed costs and delayed the election of countries in which to file applications by 18 months, as compared to the 12 months using the priority period. It is likely that at this stage the applicant will have more detailed information on the real commercial prospects for products embodying the invention in various markets and be in a position to take a more informed decision on the countries in which it will actually need protection. The application may have also been amended so that there may be fewer obstacles to grant of a patent by national patent office.

While delays in paying filing, translation and attorney fees may be very appealing for many companies, there may also be companies in fast-moving technology sectors for which a long delay in granting the patent may be undesirable. In such cases, the PCT can also be used to streamline the national processing of patents. This could be done, for example, by filing the PCT application directly (without claiming priority of an earlier national patent application) and filing a request to enter the national phase immediately upon receipt of the international search report (typically 9 months after the application was filed). Alternatively, an international preliminary examination may be demanded, allowing the application to be amended so that it is more likely that a patent will be granted by the national patent offices once the national phase has been reached.

The grant of patents under the PCT remains in the hands of national and/or regional patent offices and applicants proceeding to the national phase will have to meet national requirements for patentability, which may differ from country to country. The international search report and the international preliminary report on patentability are used by national and regional patent offices to examine the patent and, in certain patent offices, may serve as a unique basis for granting a national patent or rejecting the application. The PCT may also be used to file applications under some of the regional patent systems, namely the African Regional Intellectual Property Organization (ARIPO), the African Intellectual Property Organization (OAPI), the Eurasian Patent Organization (EAPO) and the European Patent Office (EPO).

Conclusion

The territorial nature of patents makes it important for companies to consider protecting their patents abroad if they wish to benefit from exclusive rights in foreign markets. Taking the national route for protecting inventions abroad, that is, filing patent applications in each country within the 12-months priority period, may be cumbersome for many and may represent a heavy financial burden for SMEs too early in the process of commercialization. The Patent Cooperation Treaty is, therefore, designed for companies to be able to keep their options open for as long as possible and be in a position to take informed decisions on whether and where to pursue their application. High-quality search reports and written opinions on patentability provide an opportunity for applicants to review their strategy, modify the application if necessary, in order to continue the application process based on a clearer picture of the invention's patentability.

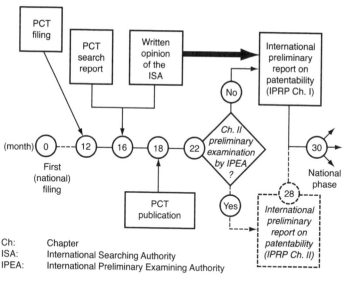

Source: WIPO 13-04-2006

figure 3 PCT timeline

6.3 European trade mark protection

OHIM at a glance

The Office of Harmonization for the Internal Market (OHIM) is the official European Union authority carrying out the procedures for the Community trade marks since 1996 and for the registered Community design from 2003. These intellectual property rights are valid in all the countries of the EU. The OHIM's purpose is to examine, register and administer Community trade marks and designs.

The Community trade mark and the Community registered design are the gateway to a single market. Their unitary nature means that formalities and management can be kept simple: a single application, a single administrative centre and a single file to be managed.

A uniform law applies to trade marks and designs, thereby providing strong and unique protection throughout the European Union.

The Community trade mark as a company asset

Trade mark protection is an increasingly important part of the marketing strategy of many businesses, particularly in a globalized marketplace where competition between companies is more prominent than ever.

With the recently enlarged European Union now boasting over 450 million inhabitants – the largest single market in the world outside China – tailor-made EU trade mark protection is proving to be a more attractive asset than ever before.

In terms of cost-effectiveness, the application fee for a Community trade mark filed electronically is €750 (approximately £520), or €900 (approximately £625) if filed by fax or by post.

If the mark proceeds to registration after examination, a separate fee of €850 (approximately £590) is then payable, meaning that ten years of unitary, EU-wide trade mark protection can be obtained for around €1,600 – just over £1,100.

In this context, the Community trade mark offers unique benefits for companies trading in the EU.

Characteristics of the Community trade mark

A Community trade mark (CTM) is a right which grants trade mark protection in one single registration across the whole of the European Union as a unified geographic territory.

Once registered, it confers on its proprietor the exclusive right to use the mark for the trading of the goods and services protected and the right to prohibit the use of identical or similar marks throughout the European Union.

It is obtained through a single administrative procedure carried out before the Office for Harmonization in the Internal Market in Alicante, Spain and, once registered, it is valid for a period of ten years from the date of filing.

As with most trade marks at national level, a CTM may consist of signs capable of being represented graphically, particularly words, designs, letters, numerals, the shape of goods or their packaging, provided that such signs are capable of distinguishing the goods or services of one undertaking from those of other undertakings.

The CTM does not replace national trade mark registrations, nor does the OHIM substitute the national industrial property offices of the member states.

CTMs can be used by businesses as an alternative to national rights, or may, as is the case in many instances, coexist alongside their already existing national trade mark registrations.

Application for a Community trade mark

A Community trade mark is obtained by filing an application at the OHIM using either the Internet-based electronic filing interface or by submitting a paper application to the Office by fax or post. The application can also be filed via any of the EU industrial property offices upon payment of an additional handling charge in most cases.

Once filed, the application undergoes an examination process to determine whether or not it will finally proceed to registration and eventually become a Community trade mark.

Following the classification of the goods and services for which Community trade mark protection is being requested, and after other administrative procedures such as checking that the formal requirements for application have been met or that all relevant documentation has been provided, the trade mark will then be examined on the basis of Absolute Grounds for Refusal, as contemplated in Article 7 of the Community Trade Mark Regulation (CTMR).

Absolute Grounds for Refusal

Absolute Grounds for Refusal is a set of conditions laid down in the CTMR which, if contravened, will lead to the refusal of the registration.

The first ground on which a trade mark can be refused Community-wide protection is if it cannot be represented graphically, as is the case for smells, holograms and some sounds, for example.

Nor can Community trade mark protection be granted to marks which, in their totality, are devoid of any distinctive character or which are descriptive or generic terms for the goods or services requested.

These are the main criteria applied by the Office when refusing a Community trade mark application, but other grounds for refusal exist, covering marks which may be considered deceptive and misleading, contrary to public morality, or three-dimensional marks whose shape is merely the result of the technical function of the object itself.

Though all Community trade mark applications are examined at one central office, the principle of refusing marks takes into account the twenty official languages spoken in the European Union, meaning that even if a particular ground for refusal applies in only one of these languages, the mark cannot be registered as a Community trade mark.

Opposition

If the OHIM decides that a mark is acceptable for registration, it will first publish it in a publicly available bulletin for a period of three months so that any parties who feel they may have prior rights to the mark can lodge an opposition to its registration before the Office.

Prior rights are, in general terms, marks which are identical to the published application, or which are so similar to it that the consumers of the same kind of products or services may be confused as to their actual trade origin.

For the OHIM to refuse an application on the basis of these prior rights, known as Relative Grounds for Refusal and laid down in Article 8 of the CTMR, it must be asked to do so by the interested prior right holder. The Office will not refuse a Community trade mark application based on Relative Grounds of its own accord, even if it is aware of the existence of such prior rights.

During this three-month period, any party, whether or not they claim rights to the mark, can make observations before the Office if they feel that there exists a legal or moral impediment to its registration. Such observations, though not legally binding on the OHIM, will be taken into account before deciding to proceed to registration.

Opposition proceedings between the Community trade mark applicant and those claiming prior rights to the mark may go on for some time, though an initial two-month 'cooling-off' period is granted to enable them to come to an amicable solution to their dispute before any intervention from OHIM.

In any case, the eventual result of such proceedings is either the refusal of the CTM application as applied for (the goods and services applied for may be limited to avoid refusal) or its acceptance for registration.

Registration

Following the conclusion of the three-month publication period, or of any opposition proceedings in favour of the CTM applicant, the mark will be registered for a period of ten years, dating from the day on which the application was filed, and renewable *ad infinitum* upon payment of a fee for subsequent periods of ten years.

National trade mark registration systems

Though Community trade mark protection is a popular and cost-effective intellectual property right for businesses operating in the European Union, the possibility of applying for a national trade mark is also an option.

Each of the member states has its own Industrial Property Office[13] through which national trade mark can be obtained: the rights they grant and the registration procedures may differ slightly form those at OHIM, and any rights conferred are limited in protection to the geographic borders of the country in question.

Such marks are also governed by the national laws of the individual member state in which they are registered and not, as is the case of Community trade marks, by a single harmonized EU Regulation.

The OHIM link to the international trade mark registration system

Where a company wishes to acquire a number of national marks, some or all of which may be for EU member states, it has the option of applying for an international registration through the World Intellectual Property Office in Geneva, Switzerland.

The OHIM is a contracting party to the Madrid Protocol on which international registrations may be based and can, therefore, be designated as a territory for protection on such a registration. Likewise, a Community trade mark may serve as the basis for an International application, as outlined in Section 6.4 below.

The international registration system offers substantial benefits in terms of centralizing the registration procedure and offers the possibility of including other, non-EU countries in a single registration certificate.

Unlike Community trade mark protection, any rights conferred using this system are subject to the individual national laws of each of the countries for which protection is sought, as is the examination procedure which decides on acceptance of the application.

Community trade mark courts

Disputes arising form illicit use of a registered Community trade mark can be brought before the Community trade mark courts which exist in each of the EU member states.

[13] Belgium, Netherlands and Luxembourg do not have separate IP offices, but rather share one single Benelux Office.

Each EU country has designated one of its national courts as a specialist CTM court, ruling on Community trade mark disputes on the basis of Community law as opposed to national law.

The decisions taken by any one CTM court are effective and binding throughout the European Union as a single unified territory.

Some statistics on community trade marks

Since the filing of the very first Community trade mark applications in April 1996, the Office has now received almost half a million more, with over 300,000 of them already registered.

Almost 65 per cent of these applications come from companies based in the European Union, with Germany and the United Kingdom leading the way, around 23 per cent from the USA and the remaining 12 per cent from over 200 countries from around the world.

In terms of industry sectors using Community trade marks as part of their marketing strategy, the electronic technologies and communication industries account for around one-third of all marks filed.

6.4 International trade mark protection: why and how?

To benefit from exclusive rights over a trade mark in foreign markets, companies must ensure that their trade mark is registered at the national or regional trade mark office. While applying individually to each trademark office may be a cumbersome and expensive process, the Madrid System for the International Registration of Marks offers a simple procedure to apply for trade mark protection in up to 78 countries through a single application, filed in one language paying only one set of fees. The Madrid System offers a useful tool for SMEs making trade mark protection in multiple jurisdictions accessible.

Exporters often realize the importance of registering their trade marks abroad once it is too late, that is, once they are faced with counterfeiters or once they are accused of infringing the rights of others. The risks of doing so are high and the consequences may be extremely costly for a company's entire export strategy.

The main function of a trade mark is that of allowing a consumer to distinguish between similar products and services. Trade marks provide information about a product and about the origin of a product. When a consumer is satisfied with a given product it is in everybody's (the consumer's and the producer's) best interest that the former may be able to identify it in order to purchase it again in the future. Trademark protection therefore enables successful exports to be easily identifiable aiding to the formation of loyal customers in foreign markets based on their trust in the products bearing certain trade marks.

Registering a trade mark in foreign markets gives a company the exclusive right to commercialize its products in those markets. This not only provides a solid basis to stop counterfeiters but also ensures that the exporting company enjoys exclusivity over what may be one of its most valuable business assets. Registering a trade mark abroad also provides the opportunity to license the trade mark to others (often in conjunction with other IP rights) or may be the basis for a company's franchising or merchandising strategy.

Protecting trade marks abroad: the Madrid System

There are essentially two ways of registering trade marks abroad. Firstly, companies may seek to register their trade mark by applying separately for registration in each of the countries (or regions) in which they have a business interest. This traditional method may be extremely cumbersome, time consuming and costly if the company intends to register in several countries (or regions). It entails getting involved with different legal requirements and languages of the respective countries, paying fees in different currencies and engaging a local trade mark agent in each jurisdiction. All these formalities have also a cost, which goes well beyond the fees charged by the Offices. Agent fees, fees for the issuance of supporting documents, for their certified translations, etc. should also be taken into account. Moreover, obtaining a portfolio of national registrations is not the end of the process. If the company changes its name or address, or if there is a change of ownership of the mark, this should be recorded in each of the respective countries, involving, once again, different legal procedures, languages and fees. A large enterprise generally has resources for these purposes while for an SME, it will simply mean that trade mark protection abroad is out of reach.

An alternative is to use the Madrid System for the International Registration of Marks. The Madrid system is governed by two treaties: the Madrid Agreement Concerning the International Registration of Marks, which dates from 1891 and the Protocol Relating to the Madrid Agreement, which came into operation in 1996. The UK is a member of the latter. The system, administered by the World Intellectual Property Organization (WIPO), provides the opportunity of registering marks in several countries by filing one single international application. It provides a legal bridge between the national and global marketplace, by facilitating the protection of trade marks in foreign jurisdictions. The resulting trade mark rights have the same effects as if the trade mark had been registered nationally in each country.

The objectives of the system are two-fold: first, to simplify the procedures with a view to protecting a mark with much lower costs and formalities; second, to facilitate the subsequent management of that protection. By providing cheaper and simpler procedures, the Madrid System makes the possibility of protecting trade marks in a large number of countries a reality for many enterprises, especially small and medium-sized enterprises, which otherwise would have never been able to afford protecting their marks internationally.

By the end of 2005, 450,000 international trademark registrations containing some 5.1 million active designations were in force in the international register. Such trade marks belonged to some 150,000 different trade mark holders (many of them SMEs). During that year, the Madrid System experienced a 13.9 per cent increase, as a record 33,000 registrations were effected, containing 356,000 designations.

With the accession of the United States and the European Community to the Protocol in 2003, the trend towards growing membership and interest in the Madrid System is continuing. In 2005, there were 78 members of the Madrid System.[14] A full list of member states is available at: http://www.wipo.int/madrid/en/.

---

[14] As the UK is a party to the Madrid Protocol and not the Madrid Agreement, applicants from the UK will only be able to use the Madrid System to apply for protection in the 66 countries and one region (the European Community) that are parties to the Protocol.

Filing applications

In order to apply for the international registration of a mark under the Protocol, a few basic requirements need to be met. In the first place, the applicant must be a national of a member state of the Madrid Union or have either a real and effective industrial and commercial establishment or a domicile in that country. Secondly, applicants must first have a national registration or application for the same mark. Applicants, therefore, cannot create a new trade mark and submit it directly for registration under the Madrid System. They must first file it nationally, in their home country, establishing what is called a 'basic mark'. The international application will be based on the basic mark and will be limited to the goods or services that were identified in the basic mark. International applications must be submitted through the national trade mark office ('office of origin').

International registrations are dependent on the basic mark for a period of five years. This means that if the basic mark is refused, opposed, or invalidated, the same will happen to the international application. Applicants, however, have the possibility to transform an international registration into a series of national applications if this were to happen. In doing so they retain the original filing date and any priority in the mark, but will face the additional costs of filing national applications.

When filing the application under the Madrid System, applicants must designate the countries in which registration is sought. Applicants from the UK can tick on any of the 66 countries that are members of the Madrid Protocol in order to apply for protection in those countries. If, at a later date, applicants require registration in other countries as a result of the expansion of their business activities into new markets, applicants are given the possibility to designate additional countries.

The costs of an international application will depend greatly on the home country of the applicant, the designated countries, the type of trade mark that is being registered (e.g. black and white or colour) and the number of classes of goods and services for which protection is sought. The website of the Madrid System has a fee calculator that enables applicants to get a quick indication of the costs depending on their specific circumstances.[15]

---

[15] See http://www.wipo.int/madrid/en/fees/

As a rule of thumb, companies seeking registration in more than two countries are likely to save money by filing their applications via the Madrid System rather than going individually to each national trade mark office.

Other than the degree of simplicity/complexity and the costs, there may be other considerations that determine a company's trade mark filing strategy abroad. These may include, for example, the time taken by a trade mark office to register a trade mark, the thoroughness of the examination undertaken by a national or regional office and the differences in requirements for registration between the different offices.

Registration

Once an international application has been filed, it is examined as to formal grounds by the International Bureau of WIPO. Once accepted by the International Bureau it is entered in the International Register, published in the *International Gazette* and the International Bureau notifies the ensuing registration to the trade mark offices of the designated countries. The offices of the designated countries have the right to refuse protection of a mark but only on substantive grounds and must do so within a limited time period of generally a maximum of 18 months. At the end of the period, if a country has not refused it, the trade mark will be deemed to be registered in that country for all the classes of goods and services for which it has been requested. For applicants, this represents a useful deadline which limits the period of uncertainty. A registration is valid for a period of 10 years and may be renewed repeatedly by paying the applicable fees.

It is important to note that the substantive examination of the mark is undertaken at the national level. Each country determines the conditions for registration and each trade mark office will examine the trade mark application according to its national rules. If a country communicates the refusal to register a trade mark within the available time limit, the applicant may choose to respond to the decision in which case hiring a local trade mark lawyer to represent the applicant before the national trade mark office will generally be required.

Managing an international registration

The simplicity in filing trade mark applications also applies to the management of the registration thereafter. For applicants, having to manage a number of trade mark registrations in different countries and in different languages may turn out to be a logistical nightmare. Through the Madrid System any future changes to the trade mark registration, such as a change in ownership or in the name or address of the trade mark holder, can be recorded in the International Register through a single simple procedural step and only paying one set of fees, instead of having the change made in each country where the trade mark has been registered.

This also applies to the renewal of the trade mark. Users of the Madrid System do not need to track multiple renewal deadlines and file multiple renewal applications but can renew the application through a single form submitted to the International Bureau of WIPO. As of April 2006, renewals can also be done online.

Conclusion

Companies that intend to export their products or services to other countries or wish to license their trade mark(s) to be exploited by others in those countries, securing exclusive rights over their trade marks is key. The national route of filing trade mark applications in each national trade mark office may be a suitable strategy when the number of countries is limited. But as soon as the number begins to grow, the complexity of the process becomes evident. The Madrid System offers an attractive route for SMEs as they can register their trade marks abroad through a single application form, in one language, paying a single set of fees. Unless the trade mark is refused, they do not need to hire a national trade mark agent in each country and can therefore save significant costs. The subsequent management and renewal of the registration is also significantly easier and cheaper making trade mark protection abroad accessible for SMEs.

Further information on the Madrid System for the International Registration of Marks is available at: http://www.wipo.int/madrid/en/

6.5 The Community design

The national design laws of the European member states have been harmonized and brought into line with Directive 98/71/EC to create a Community design.

The Regulation on Community Designs was adopted by the Council on 12 December 2001 (EC) (n°6/2002).

The European Commission then adopted on 22 October 2002 a Regulation of its own giving the OHIM the administrative tools it needed to operate the system, such as the registration and cancellation of designs and the procedure for appeals (EC) (n°2245/2002).

Finally, a second Commission Regulation adopted on 19 December 2002 set the fees payable for the registration of Community designs (EC) (n°2246/2002).

A Community design automatically offers protection to a design across all member states, provided that the design fulfils the necessary criteria; this protection extends to any product or part of a product incorporating the design or a substantially similar design.

A Community design may be registered or unregistered. Either way, there are three essential prerequisites to obtaining and maintaining a Community design: the design must fall within the specific definition of a 'design', be new and have individual character.

Registered Community designs

To obtain a registered Community design, a proprietor must apply to register the design with the OHIM, which then processes and administers the application. OHIM takes around three months and quotes a fee of €350 to register one design. OHIM will conduct an examination to ensure compliance with certain formalities, but will not look at whether a design is new or has individual character.

A registered Community design provides the proprietor with an exclusive right to prevent infringement across the European Community. A single registration will give protection for an initial term of five years, capable of renewal for up to four further five-year periods – 25 years in total – on payment of renewal fees.

Proprietors can register several designs under a single application as long as they fall within the same class of the International Classification for Industrial Designs. A proprietor that has made a multiple registration will be able to treat each design as an individual right for licensing and infringement purposes.

The register

All registered Community designs are published in the Community Designs Bulletin that exists in electronic format only, as a multilingual edition in the 20 official languages of the European Union. The Bulletin can be consulted at http://oami.eu. int/en/design/bull.htm.

The Community Designs Bulletin may be searched by entering text relating either to the name and address of the applicant, representative or designer, to the matching file or registration numbers, to dates or indication of products for which design protection is sought.

Unregistered Community designs

An unregistered Community design right arises automatically from the date on which the design was first made available to the public within the Community. Provided the design satisfies the relevant criteria, there is no need to register the design or to notify OHIM for the right to accrue. The right confers on its holder a right to prevent copying for a limited period of three years. There is no scope for renewal.

This simplicity does, however, have its downside because in practice the holder of the UCD may encounter serious problems proving that the protection exists.

What constitutes a design?

A 'design' is defined as 'the appearance of the whole or a part of a product resulting from the features of, in particular, the lines, contours, colours, shape, texture or materials of the product or its ornamentation'.

Almost every company will have created or will use some form of design capable of falling within this definition, which is very broad and now includes logos, graphic symbols and icons. The protection has widened from attaching to the product itself to attaching to the appearance or design incorporated into any product, and can apply to a whole product or to a part or feature of a product. The categories of product have also been extended to include any industrial or handicraft item and to include packaging and get-up.

Is it new?

For registered Community designs, to be 'new', the design must not have been made available to the public anywhere in the world (not just the European Community) prior to the date on which the application for registration was filed, unless the disclosure was made under confidentiality obligations. Being made available to the public includes the design being published or used in other products, exhibited or disclosed in some other way. For unregistered Community designs, to be novel the design must not have been made available to the public in the Community before the date on which the design was first made available to the public by the proprietor.

However, registered Community designs are now subject to a grace period of 12 months from earliest disclosure to the public to application. Disclosure of the design to the public within this grace period will not preclude the design from being capable of registration. This is particularly helpful where a proprietor wants to trial a product or a design publicly or to exhibit it, to test its commercial market or viability prior to filing an application and incurring that expense.

Does it have individual character?

A design has 'individual character' if the overall impression it creates on the informed user is, in essence, that he or she has not seen it all before; that is, the impression created by this design or product differs from the overall impression produced on such a user by any design which has been made available to the public. In assessing the character, the extent to which the designer had free rein will be considered. Those features of a product which are dictated solely by the product's technical function or which need to fit with other component parts cannot be considered designs capable of protection; but equally if those parameters leave little scope for individuality or significant difference between designs, the degree of individual character required for the design to pass the test will be lower. Aesthetic considerations and 'eye appeal' are no longer relevant; nor does the design have to be capable of industrial application.

Advantages of a registered Community design

There are certainly advantages to having a registered Community design rather than an unregistered Community design, particularly where the design is intended to have a degree of longevity or is to be market tested before being used or marketed. A registered Community design gives protection to the design for up to 25 years compared to three years for an unregistered design, and a registered design has the benefit of the 12-month grace period for public disclosure before an application is made.

A registered Community design gives an exclusive right, across all member states, in relation to infringement. An unregistered design merely gives a right to prevent copying and, as there is no registration requirement, is harder to police and defend. So if a third party has conceived of an identical design acting independently, it will not have infringed the design as there has been no copying of it.

A registered Community design allows for one Europe-wide system of application with a central administrative body (OHIM), with filings at a designated cost and in a single language. It is also important to bear in mind that it is the design which is capable of registration, so it is no longer necessary to make separate registrations for each product to which the design will be applied. There is also the possibility of filing several designs under one application and of filing the application but deferring publication for up to 30 months to avoid disclosure to competitors.

In relation to both registered and unregistered Community designs, when it comes to infringement there is a degree of latitude in selecting the forum in which to bring an action, with pan-European enforcement and protection measures available, including interim injunctive relief.

Protection

To be fully effective, any strategy that seeks to exploit the opportunities offered by the wider scope of these design rights should also provide for taking measures to protect them.

Each member state has designated a specialist court to hear cases relating to Community designs. The Community design court in any given member state has jurisdiction over infringing actions anywhere in the European Community and may grant interim injunctions, damages, delivery up and other protective measures in any other member state. Jurisdiction is determined by reference to domicile or establishment within the European Community; failing that, the Spanish courts will take jurisdiction (as the domicile of OHIM).

Conclusion

In assessing and reviewing a company's portfolio and developing strategies for the protection of IP rights, the full range of assets and options must be considered, but the previously humble design right ought now to feature a little more prominently within that programme.

Community designs are not a replacement for other Community rights and national protection, but their existence can add value to a qualifying design, and can allow that value to be more readily quantified and exploited across an expanding European market in a relatively inexpensive and cost-effective manner.

Outlook

EU Accession to the Hague Agreement

In perspective 2006 sees the EU Accession to the Hague agreement, building literally a bridge between the Community system (RCD) and the international design registration system of the World Intellectual Property Organization (WIPO). That would allow users to file their design simultaneously in no less than 53 countries, of which 38 countries are members of the International Design System and the other 15 are signatories to the Geneva Act including Singapore, Korea, Turkey and Switzerland that came into force on 23 December 2003. The OHIM has started internal preparations in order to contribute to a smooth operation of the international registration system, if this accession is finally adopted.

This simplified procedure would lead to a saving of costs: there would no longer be a need to provide translations of the documents, to keep watch on the different deadlines for renewal of a great number of national registrations and to pay a series of national fees and fees to agents in different countries.

The creation of a link between the Community design system and the Hague arrangement would benefit a wide range of industrial sectors, in particular textiles, furniture, cars, jewellery and mobile phones.

For more information see: http://www.wipo.int/hague/en/

E-business

E-filing enables clients to apply for a registered Community design online. The advantages are:

- receipt of real-time confirmation
- on-line verification to assure error-free filing and secure your filing date
- speedy entry into the registration process
- ready access to the user-friendly online help

More information and detailed instructions on how to register a design?

The full text of the Regulation is available at:

http://www.europa.eu.int/comm/internal_market/en/indprop/design/index.htm

Further practical details are available on the OHIM website at: http://oami.eu.int/

6.6 International copyright protection

Through the UK's membership of various international conventions, a copyright work created in the UK is automatically protected in most parts of the world. This can be very beneficial to a person who creates a copyright work, that is, worldwide protection for the creation without having to do anything.

The UK is a member of several international conventions in this field, notably the Berne Convention for the Protection of Literary and Artistic Works and the Universal Copyright Convention (UCC). Copyright material created by UK nationals or residents is protected in each member country of the conventions by the national law of that country. Most countries belong to at least one of the conventions, including all the western European countries, the USA and Russia. Protection overseas can also arise from obligations in the agreement on Trade Related Aspects of Intellectual Property Rights (TRIPS), which forms part of the World Trade Organization (WTO) Agreement.

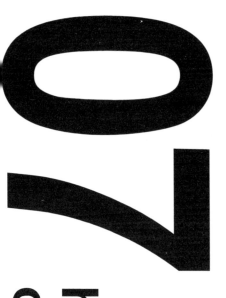

07

help from others

In this chapter you will learn:
- about NESTA and MAS
- how inventor clubs can help you
- how to use invention promoters
- about business support from the Design Council

7.1 National Endowment for Science, Technology and the Arts

Overview

NESTA, the National Endowment for Science, Technology and the Arts (www.nesta.org.uk), is working to transform the UK's capacity for innovation. NESTA's work is underpinned by a fundamental view that innovation and the exploitation of ideas will fuel long-term economic and social progress in the UK and are essential ingredients for our competitive edge in the global market. NESTA invests in all stages of the innovation process, backing new ideas and funding new ventures that stimulate entrepreneurship.

NESTA is working towards being the single most potent catalyst for innovation in the UK and its strong evidence base helps to influence policy. Its partnerships and networks accelerate the process of innovation. NESTA's pioneering models of investment are being adopted by organizations throughout the UK.

Current review and the new NESTA direction

NESTA's new direction emerged from an understanding of:

- the key drivers of an effective national innovation system
- the UK's current innovation performance
- what innovators need to realize their potential
- the levers for policy and practice change.

NESTA's new direction has a clear and renewed vision of a UK leading the world in the application of knowledge, creativity and enterprise.

The ambition for NESTA is for the organization to be instrumental in bringing about a more dynamic and successful environment for innovation in the UK. NESTA's mission is to *transform the UK's capacity for innovation.*

NESTA has the following aims to deliver:

1 *To galvanize the UK's entrepreneurial potential and spirit of enquiry*: NESTA wants to encourage a more can-do, risk-taking culture in the UK, and to enhance innovative thinking in talented people.

2 *To increase the quantity of private sector investment at seed stage*: NESTA will boost the availability of funds to enable early stage innovations to get off the ground.

3 *To enrich and strengthen innovation policy in the UK:* NESTA wants innovation policy to respond more effectively to the dynamics of innovation, addressing weaknesses in provision and increasing the funding for high-impact initiatives

These aims are consonant with the remit provided for NESTA in the National Lottery Act (1998), which charges NESTA to 'support and promote talent, innovation and creativity in the fields of science, technology and the arts', through supporting talented individuals, the exploitation of new ideas, and public appreciation of science, technology and the arts.

Three key dimensions of the strategy

NESTA focuses on the three aspects of innovation:

- human dimension
- finance dimension
- policy dimension.

Human: Innovation needs creative thinkers capable of problem solving and aligning knowledge and expertise with the needs and opportunities of the future. It needs entrepreneurs who will take risks, set up ventures and drive them forward. It requires networks, sources of advice and mentoring. It needs an interdisciplinary approach to finding innovative solutions.

Finance: The search for early stage pre-revenue seed financing is a painful one in the UK. The landscape is fragmented and traditional sources of finance are moving to later stage activities. There is a role for NESTA to absorb levels of early stage risk and create a platform for private sector investment to follow. NESTA provides seed capital and tailored support for the early stage commercialization of innovation. NESTA will act as a catalyst, deploying public finance strategically, so as to foster innovation.

Policy: NESTA's national mission is to ensure that innovation has a fertile climate in which to thrive and a fiscal and regulatory environment that encourages business formation and survival. Innovation also needs a culture that respects and celebrates entrepreneurship and risk-taking, and facilitates the skills that enable possibility to become reality.

Programme outlines

The human dimension focuses on developing the skills and attitudes required for innovation to flourish. It gives rise to three programmes:

1 *Incubating Innovation.* Learning how to nurture enterprise capability and entrepreneurial skills by developing scalable models of experimental learning. This is enhanced with the dissemination and learning from NESTA's interventions and supporting best practice across the UK and internationally. The focus of activity will concentrate primarily on building the enterprise capability of young people and engaging with the curricula across the UK.

2 *Innovation Challenges.* Initiating issue-based challenges which enable new forms of interdisciplinary collaboration supported with the establishment of an Innovation Challenge Fund that enables NESTA to develop potential challenges (with the public or private sector) focused on solving a seemingly intractable problem or future social issues. NESTA brings together interdisciplinary teams; talented scientists, technologists and artists capable of combining knowledge and applications in new ways. NESTA facilitates collaborative approaches, team working and interdisciplinary thinking to generate ideas and solutions. NESTA explores tests and learns from different approaches to collaborative working and provide a series of high profile, issue-based platforms and campaigns which raise public awareness, engage society in scientific developments, products and product or service design.

3 *Innovation Networks.* NESTA seeks to maximize the potential of innovation networks across the UK. Networks play a pivotal role in accelerating the process of innovation and they facilitate knowledge sharing across sectors and disciplines providing access to expertise and finance. An innovation system needs rich, diverse networks and clusters in order to be self-sustaining and remain dynamic.

The finance dimension. NESTA acts as a catalyst for the capital and skills associated with the UK's pre-innovative start-ups and gives rise to two programmes that are integrally linked. NESTA does not invest funding unless there is a clear management and strategic structure in place with the potential investee:

• *Seed Fund.* The unique properties of an endowment allow for a different attitude to risk and time than traditional investment funds. NESTA's Seed Fund acts as a catalyst and develops relationships with the early stage investment community creating the leverage for more liquidity, better and higher-quality deal flow and building models of best practice. NESTA's function should not be understood as just one of the key suppliers of capital, but rather as a partner who can leverage the activities of other players, helping them build increasing numbers of successful early stage companies at innovative pre-revenue early stage businesses. NESTA will not compete directly for deal flow with early stage investors or act as yet another early stage investor. NESTA leverages third-party resources, supports the effective capitalization of companies and supports and enables the best early stage entrepreneurs and investors thus creating a link between early stage investors and venture capitalists.

- *Mentoring*. This enhances the growth of innovative businesses by supporting entrepreneurs and NESTA seeks to make more businesses investment-ready propositions for second round funding by early stage investors and venture capitalists. The mentor's principal responsibilities will be strategic and business planning including exit strategy, intellectual property and confidentiality, good business practices and compliance matters, market issues and route to markets. The programme develops powerful partnerships and networks across the investment community.

The policy dimension. Policy and research. The overarching goal of the policy and research programme is to assist NESTA to have a transformative impact on UK innovation policy and practice.

- *Engagement* is achieved by generating new knowledge and insights about innovation and engaging policymakers and practitioners in constructive dialogue and proposing new solutions to innovative policy and practice issues. The programme will focus on deepening understanding about innovation capacity and potential, examining the policy implications, and seeking to influence policy.
- *Intelligence*: the programme positions NESTA as a thought leader on innovation by becoming an acknowledged resource on innovation thinking and providing intelligence on policy developments abroad and successful support programmes. NESTA also publishes and disseminates research on key aspects of innovation practice and analyses of innovation policy.

7.2 Inventor clubs

'None of us are as smart as all of us.' (Japanese Proverb)

Walking through the door of an inventor club for the first time, you could be in for a pleasant surprise. Inventor clubs are fast becoming vibrant networking organizations where invention and innovation is encouraged, fostered and promoted through lively discussion and support.

Like anything in life, you get out what you put in. Inventor clubs depend on their members as one of their most valuable assets. After all, the best people to learn from are those who have already had to learn the pitfalls of invention and innovation: the importance of protecting your ideas, making prototypes, patents, copyrights, trade marks, design registration, marketing and the whole complicated process of making your new product a success. Constructive criticism is somehow easier to stomach from another inventor who has been through the mill and you may even be encouraged on your way by some very positive feedback as well.

Novice inventors can have a very different attitude from experienced inventors, believing that their invention is worth millions and have heard stories of how an idea can make them very rich very quickly. This can result in them asking for unreasonable royalty or lump sum payments for their inventions. Meeting other inventors who have 'been there and done that', the reality sinks in but does not dampen the determination of the novice. Decide what you want to achieve and there will doubtless be someone there who has already climbed those stairs.

The entrepreneurial spirit is alive and kicking as today's inventors are becoming more and more aware of the business skills necessary to ensure their idea becomes a commercial success. As well as the lone inventor, clubs attract representatives of industry, investors, professional service providers and universities, who all come together to share experiences and offer mutual support and opportunities.

Traditionally, inventors in the UK are stereotyped as laughable crackpots who sit in their sheds coming up with whacky, impractical ideas destined for nothing but failure. However, the moment an inventor has a great commercial breakthrough, perception changes and success is celebrated and recognized and their story becomes one of achievement against the odds.

How different things are for those who make the bold step of joining a club. Individual creativity is nurtured and respected by inventor clubs and members take each other's contribution seriously, offering guidance and sharing support and encouragement. Without this fundamental support structure in place during the early stages of development, many UK inventors would lose heart and their inventions could be lost or exploited overseas.

The range of personalities and characters at inventor clubs is very diverse: a vast range of people have had that spark of an idea or a solution to a problem and are all looking for various kinds of assistance. People who attend inventor clubs value each other for their potential rather than their background and this lively mix can make for animated discussions and valuable exchange of experiences and expertise.

Invention is often done in secret and being an inventor can sometimes be very lonely, not knowing who to talk to or where to go for advice. Family and friends do not always share the same enthusiasm, but in a club there is a very strong spirit of camaraderie which is welcoming to a novice inventor and attracts experienced inventors to come back.

So, apart from the obvious networking potential and emotional support, what else can an inventor club offer?

Being a member of a club can give you not only the opportunity to open doors that would normally be closed, but also the guidance and expertise once you have got through.

Most inventor clubs hold their regular meetings early in an evening, aware that many inventors starting out are already in employment and have day jobs. Some clubs organize speakers on specific topics such as protecting your ideas, licensing, manufacturing, marketing and attracting finance or invite successful inventors along to tell their story. These meetings give plenty of opportunities to throw out questions or problems to the speaker and to the group for input. Meetings are generally followed by a more informal get-together over a drink and some food in a local pub.

Inventor clubs issue newsletters, an easy way to receive up-to-date information on topical issues in the world of inventions, forthcoming awards, competitions and exhibitions. TV companies and the media are regular contributors, using this conduit to reach inventors.

Some clubs provide free or heavily subsidized support services specifically designed for individual inventors and innovators. These can consist of one-to-one advice sessions, with experts in manufacturing, intellectual property, licensing, marketing, design and prototyping and (aware of the lack of funding which affects many inventors) grants available and one-day seminars arranged for novice inventors. These provide inventors with step-by-step guidelines to assist in understanding the key elements to be considered in turning their idea into a business.

Most inventor clubs have websites; this offers their members the opportunity to promote themselves and their inventions to the media and also for business opportunities. For an inventor who has a product to sell advertising on a club website is another possible outlet for sales.

Websites can include forums and notice boards for discussions and are good sounding boards for problem solving and seeking advice.

Inventor clubs often participate at exhibitions in the UK and overseas. Exhibiting under the umbrella of a club can not only reduce costs and help with resources but they can offer guidance on exhibiting including assistance in producing press releases and promotional literature. Novice inventors are often unsure of how to follow up on contacts made at exhibitions; clubs can offer advice on the importance of following up on these leads and on how to deal with distributors, manufacturers, potential licensees and investors.

Some clubs have become intermediaries between inventors and industry. Individual inventors and SMEs come up with inventions, which they do not have the capacity or resource to develop and exploit. This may mean attracting the interest of, and negotiating with an entity of some size. In the initial stage of contact between the parties, there is often difficulty on both sides in getting a constructive dialogue established. Very often, the inventor is understandably keen to explain and extol the technical merit of the idea while the potential partner is considerably more interested in the commercial considerations and profit generation.

To expand awareness some clubs are arranging workshops targeted at businesses and professionals to understand intellectual property and its value.

The structure and operation of clubs in the UK vary. Some have been set up by inventors and membership is only for inventors. Some encourage professionals as members and this diverse membership allows an inventor to gain many different perspectives. But all clubs have a strong bond in their knowledge of where to get cost-effective assistance and, in contrast, which companies are operating 'invention promotion' scams.

Some clubs ask members and guests to sign a confidentiality agreement for attendance at meetings. These agreements may protect you from non-disclosure of your idea, but be sure to read these agreements and see who is responsible for any breach of confidentiality.

Membership of an inventor club often entails a modest subscription, a small financial outlay to gain access to a group of like-minded people and an invaluable network.

Unlike Groucho Marx, who famously said: 'I don't want to belong to any club that accepts people like me as members', inventors find that the cooperative effort of being a member of a club helps them to achieve their goal.

The day of the lone inventor is not over; many successful businesses are still being instigated by inventions from individuals. If you have an idea and your first port of call is an inventor club, you will not be disappointed.

Representatives of UK inventor clubs meet and correspond regularly to share information, giving greater cross-fertilizing on services and further expanding the network to benefit their members. To find out about inventor clubs in the UK and overseas and the services they provide visit www.ideas21.co.uk.

For a list of forthcoming events, seminars, workshops, exhibitions, clinics, meetings, training programmes, competitions and awards relating to invention, innovation and intellectual property visit www.innovationcalendar.co.uk.

7.3 Step-by-step guide to using invention promoters

Do you think you have a great idea for a new product or service? You are not alone.

Every year thousands of people try to develop their ideas and market them commercially. Some people use the services of invention promotion firms to help evaluate, develop and market their idea. The 'help' of some promoters can be a costly mistake.

Invention promotion firms offer to help you evaluate, develop and market your idea but first you have to be clear about whether you have made the right choice of firm. Some inventors find themselves broke and without proper intellectual property protection after using the services of a rogue invention promoter.

The facts are:

- few inventions ever make it to the marketplace
- although a patent can provide valuable protection for a successful invention, getting a patent doesn't necessarily increase the chances of commercial success.

There's great satisfaction in developing a new product or service and in getting a patent. But when it comes to determining market potential, inventors should proceed with caution as they try to avoid falling for the sweet-sounding promises of a fraudulent promotion firm.

The pitch

Advertisements for invention promotion firms appear on television, radio and the Internet, and in newspapers and magazines. These adverts target independent inventors with offers of free information on how to patent and market their inventions. However, often the information is about the promoter.

After giving your invention a preliminary review, a firm might tell you it needs to do a market evaluation of your idea for a fee that can be several hundred pounds. Many questionable firms don't do any genuine research or market evaluations. The 'research' is bogus, and the 'positive' reports are mass produced in an effort to sell clients additional invention promotion and marketing services.

Fraudulent invention promotion firms don't offer an honest appraisal of the merit, technical feasibility or market potential of an invention.

Some invention promotion firms may also offer a contract in which they agree to help you market and license your invention to manufacturers. Unscrupulous promoters may require you to pay a fee of several thousand pounds in advance.

Reputable licensing agents don't rely on large advance fees. Rather, they depend on royalties from the successful licensing of client inventions. So few inventions make it to the marketplace that they are choosy about which ideas or inventions they pursue. If a firm is enthusiastic about the market potential of your idea – but charges you a fee in advance – consider taking your business elsewhere.

Using invention promoters

Good invention promoters will reject most of the inventions pitched to them, only taking on those inventions in which they have faith. The less reputable promoters heap praise on inventors to encourage them to part with cash for hopeless ideas. If the promoter is leaving the bulk of the financial risk with the inventor then perhaps they don't believe that success is likely.

There are a number of important points to consider before you employ an invention promotion company:

1 Do you need the services of an invention promoter? Try to do as much research for yourself as possible. The Patent Office website www.patent.gov.uk and the Intellectual Property Portal can provide you with lots of background information on patents, trade marks, design registrations and copyright. Using an invention promoter is just one of the many ways to market your new products or ideas.

2 If you decide to approach an invention promoter, make sure that details of your invention are kept confidential. Disclosing how the invention works without a confidentiality agreement will harm any future patent application.

3 Before you hand over any money or sign an agreement, ask the promoter about the stages involved in promoting your product such as research, marketing and licensing, and any associated costs.

4 Remember that once a dishonest company has your money, it's unlikely you will ever get it back.

5 As with any company that you might employ to work for you, check the promoter's credentials. Request evidence of their skills, expertise and success rate. You could ask to see their references from previous clients.

6 Most good invention promotion firms would have rejected lots of ideas in the first assessment stage as not being commercially viable. Find out what percentage the firm has rejected as evidence of how seriously they look into inventions.

7 If they offer services such as a patent search or market assessment, see if they provide these for the countries in which you would like to market your invention. You can check the competitiveness of their patent search costs by comparison with the Patent Office's Search and Advisory Service. For further information contact the Patent Office Search and Advisory service on 01633 811010 or commercialsearches@ patent.gov.uk.

8 Make sure that their search is comprehensive because an invention must be new if a patent is to succeed. Over 30 million published patent applications from around the world can be viewed for free from the esp@cenet patent database on the Patent Office website. This will tell you if your 'new' idea has been invented before! For further information contact esp@cenet at www.espacenet.com.

9 Check for evidence that they know the sector for your product and have contacts with manufacturers. Ask for proof if they claim to represent manufacturers on the look-out for new product ideas.

10 Ask if the firm offers the services of a patent agent or patent attorney and if those people are registered. The Chartered Institute of Patent Agents (CIPA) is the professional body for patent agents in the UK. Its aim is to increase awareness and understanding of the innovation process by providing a basic information pack and free clinics, and by arranging talks or seminars when appropriate. CIPA members help inventors to obtain protection, not only in patents, but also in trade marks, designs and copyright. For further information call CIPA on 020 7405 9450, e-mail mail@cipa.org.uk or visit their website: www.cipa.org.uk.

11 Direct any complaints on invention promoters to the Office of Fair Trading for investigation. OFT can be contacted at www.oft.gov.uk or via Consumer Direct on 08454 04 05 06.

If, at the end of all this, you are happy with the evidence and do wish to enter into a contract, ensure that it contains all the terms you agreed to – verbal and written – before you sign. If possible you should seek legal advice.

For more information about patent, trade marks, design registrations and copyright, visit the Patent Office website at www.patent.gov.uk or the Intellectual Property Portal at www.intellectual-property.gov.uk or ring 08459 500 505.

7.4 Manufacturing Advisory Service

Introduction

The Manufacturing Advisory Service (MAS) is a Department of Trade and Industry led initiative aimed at improving the performance of the UK manufacturing industry. It is a national scheme covering England and Wales.

Support is geared towards small and medium enterprises (SMEs), start-up companies, and helping designers.

Its core aims are to improve the levels of quality, reduce unit costs, and improve the on-time delivery of manufactured goods and services. In short, it is charged with helping SMEs to deliver excellent products and services to new and existing customers and markets.

MAS is also interested in promoting manufacturing in the UK, and helping to support manufacturing in terms of publicity, promotion, and attracting high calibre individuals and suppliers.

The service is delivered nationally through a series of regional centres, aligned with, and supported by, the Regional Development Agencies (RDAs). In many cases, the RDAs have additional support goals to the national goals outlined above. Such goals include help with safeguarding jobs, creating new jobs, and support for minority and ethnic groups.

Essentially, it offers a subsidized support service for the initial stages of engagement, which allows SMEs access to services which might otherwise be precluded.

The delivery team is made up of experienced professionals drawn from a variety of manufacturing industry sectors, and with extensive manufacturing skills and practical expertise. It is therefore a unique service, since it is delivered by manufacturers for manufacturers.

An additional and important part of the MAS remit is the active promotion of the importance of manufacturing to the UK economy, as a career choice, and the dissemination and implementation of best practice.

The London MAS has a particularly close link with the Patent Office.

Practical support

MAS offers practical support to designers and manufacturers in terms of material selection, design for manufacture, design for assembly, and the liaison between designer and manufacturer. It can also help with prototyping, and getting the product into the market.

A free helpline is offered by all MAS regions.

MAS specialists will also attend seminars, workshops, conferences and exhibitions in order to offer face-to-face practical advice to designers and manufacturers.

In many regions, MAS has close working relationships with colleges and universities, and can often help access unknown sources of information, knowledge and capability, as well as leading edge research and technology transfer.

MAS regularly run, sponsor, and support many workshops and events which promote leading-edge design, innovation, and the embodiment of creativity.

We also help and advise on project management, new product introduction, routes to market, and product development.

For more information contact the national centre on 0845 6589600 or visit the website at www.mas.dti.gov.uk.

Intellectual property

MAS understands and respects the importance of IP support and protection.

The use of non-disclosure agreements is well established, and so designers and manufacturers can have confidence that right from the initial engagement with MAS, all ideas and content are fully protected and secure.

MAS works closely with support agencies and partners, including the Patent Office to actively promote the use and benefits of IP.

MAS London, for example, runs a regular, free, advisory clinic for designers and manufacturers co-located with partners such as ideas21 (see Section 7.2), who offer free access to first level IP advice and guidance.

We often see the early potential in ideas and products, and can assist in the brokerage of the necessary support.

There are some excellent fact sheets available at: http://www.mas.dti.gov.uk/pluto-resources/1130402570820.pdf

Case studies

A-Leg-Gro PED – E. and S. Pillinger

Suzanne Cheetam Pillinger was born in the north of England. She studied at the Paris Conservatoire and has given recitals throughout Europe, the USA and Japan. She has played with the BBC Symphony Orchestra, the London Sinfonietta, the Bayerischer Rundfunk Orchestra and has made numerous recordings and live broadcasts for the BBC.

Suzanne is a distinguished piano teacher and has taught privately for many years.

Her involvement in the education of very young beginners and her frustration at the inability of these younger pupils to benefit from an early introduction to the pedal inspired her, in collaboration with her husband, Edward, to design the 'A-Leg-Gro PED' (piano pedal extension device).

This brilliant teaching aid consists of an adjustable footrest which supports both feet comfortably and incorporates an independently adjustable pedal which activates the piano pedal from varying heights.

The development of good posture in the early years of piano playing is vitally important; this is impossible to achieve if a child's feet do not reach the ground comfortably. The A-Leg-Gro PED provides this necessary support with a firm platform which can be easily adjusted as the child grows.

The company got a patent for it but for the UK only – although they contacted the Patent Office who gave them helpful advice, they elected to handle all the form filling themselves, without fully appreciating the steps they should have taken to protect their product.

A few years on and they were successfully exporting some of the products to Korea – a buyer there was selling them in his shop. The relationship was working well, until a rival saw one, copied it and promptly put it into production, effectively cutting off the Korean market to them.

Worse still, the same thing has subsequently happened in the United States – where the company which is producing them are claiming not only to be the originators of the product, but cheekily warn potential customers to be wary of imported copies!

MAS has put them in touch with a patent lawyer who has given them some sound advice subsequently, but it would have been much better if they'd gone down that route first!

For more information contact ped@pillingermouthpieces.co.uk.

Aqualogix – Ashton Industrial – Barry East

This wonderful device can help save lives. Every day 3,000 children die in the developing world as a direct result of drinking polluted water, but this could become a thing of the past, if this device is as successful as it deserves to be.

This small, portable device requires no external power source, running from a small hand or foot pump, is self-contained, and could be carried in a rucksack. It is estimated that the finished unit will cost approximately £1,500.

It can filter 5,000 litres of water per day from contaminated rivers, lakes, and wells. This is enough water to sustain 1,000 people a day. What makes the system unique is that it uses a mechanical, chemical free filtration system, which can filter out harmful bacteria, virus colonies, parasitic worms, and suspended particles, without depleting the necessary life-supporting minerals from the water. The resultant water is clean, fresh and healthy – and meets the World Health Organization's standards for drinking water.

Such a unit could be used for disaster relief work as well

MAS was able to assist Ashton Industrial and its designer Barry East with schemes and ideas for the look of the final unit, materials for construction, and help evaluate the prototype unit, which included first-hand sampling of the clean water produced.

MAS was also able to broker a meeting on the inherent IPR interests in the unit with patent lawyers, which has now resulted in successful patent applications. This is one project where the UK design team needs IPR protection.

Initial units have now been donated by the manufacturers for extended field trials in Malawi, Africa, and Guyana, South America. They are continuing to seek sponsorship and support for this project. Sadly to date, none of the major UK-based charities have been able to support the project.

Significant support has however been forthcoming from the DDA – the Defence Diversification Authority.

For more information contact: sashton@ashton-industrial.com and see http://www.dda.gov.uk/publications/docs/NEWsletter Sept05.pdf.

7.5 DTI business support solutions

In business you make your own success but government could help to overcome some of the barriers you face. Each year the Department of Trade & Industry (DTI) invests over £400 million assisting businesses through grants, loans and subsidized consultancy.

There are a range of products and services available from the DTI that assist businesses in developing innovative ideas and their intellectual property, which include the following.

Knowledge transfer networks

This is a grant to bring together businesses, universities and others with an interest in technology applications.

A knowledge transfer network is a single national overarching network in a specific field of technology or business application. It brings together a variety of organizations, such as businesses (suppliers and customers), universities, research and technology organizations, the finance community and other intermediaries who will provide a range of activities and initiatives to enable the exchange of knowledge and stimulation of innovation amongst this community.

The objective of a knowledge transfer network is to improve the UK's innovation performance by increasing the breadth and depth of the knowledge transfer of technology into UK-based businesses and by accelerating the rate at which this process occurs.

Collaborative research and development

This is funding for collaborative R&D projects.

The objective of collaborative research and development is to assist the industry and research communities to work together on research and development projects in strategically important areas of science, engineering and technology, from which successful new products, processes and services can emerge. It also primes the flow of the latest knowledge and thinking from the UK's science, engineering and technology base to business. Collaborative research and development projects must involve two or more collaborators, at least one of which is from industry.

The technology programme supports three categories of research:

Pure or oriented basic research

This encompasses both experimental or theoretical work undertaken primarily to acquire new knowledge of the underlying foundations of phenomena and observable facts, without any particular application or use in view. Funding support will favour oriented basic research over pure basic research. By oriented basic research we mean research carried out with the expectation that it will produce a broad base of knowledge likely to form the background to the solution of recognized or expected current or future problems or possibilities.

Applied research

This encompasses original investigation undertaken in order to acquire new knowledge directed primarily towards a specific practical aim or objective. This type of research may involve the creation of a project to take forward the results of a basic research programme.

Experimental development

This encompasses systematic work, drawing on existing knowledge gained from research and practical experience, that is directed to producing new materials, products and devices; or to installing new processes, systems and services; or to improving substantially those already produced or installed.

Knowledge transfer partnerships

These are a grant to transfer and embed knowledge into a business from the UK knowledge base via a strategic project.

All approved knowledge transfer partnerships are part-funded by the Government and can enable your business to work with a university, college or research organization that has expertise relevant to your business and can help you increase profitability. There is expertise in the UK's universities, colleges and research organizations that could be of value to your business in developing new products, services and processes.

Knowledge transfer partnerships are designed to help you access this expertise and bring it into your business by working in partnership with academics or researchers.

How does it work?

With the help of a specialist knowledge transfer partnership consultant, you will identify a university, college or research organization that has the right expertise for your business.

Together you will then define and agree a project that will enable you to draw on their expertise and apply it to your business. The agreed project could be for any length of time between one and three years, with the overall aim of helping your business make a step change in an area that you have identified as high priority for your business.

What kind of businesses can take part?

Businesses of all sizes in most industries and commercial sectors can take part. There are some limitations on the type of project and the sectors that can be supported.

Grants for research and development

Grants for research and development are designed to help individuals and small and medium-sized businesses research and develop technologically innovative products and processes.

The following help is available:

- **Micro projects** are simple low cost development projects lasting no longer than 12 months. The output should be a simple prototype of a novel or innovative product or process. A grant of up to £20,000 is available to businesses with fewer than 10 employees.

- **Research projects** typically involve planned research or critical investigation lasting between 6 and 18 months. The result of the project could be new scientific or technical knowledge that may be useful in developing a new product or process. A grant of up to £75,000 is available to businesses with fewer than 50 employees.

- **Development projects** involve the shaping of industrial research into a pre-production prototype of a technologically innovative product or industrial process. A grant of up to £200,000 is available for businesses with fewer than 250 employees.

- **Exceptional projects** involve technology developments which have higher costs. These projects are likely to generate much wider economic benefits and must have strategic importance for a technology or industrial sector. A grant of up to £500,000 is available to businesses with fewer than 250 employees.

- **Regional development agencies** – Grants are also available from regional development agencies (RDAs). RDAs are responsible for appraising applications and deciding which projects to support in their region. They also pay grant claims and monitor the progress of supported projects.

For more information on the business support service offered by your local RDA please visit:

Advantage West Midlands: http://www.advantagewm.co.uk/

East Midlands Development Agency: http://www.emda.org.uk/

East of England Development Agency: http://www.eeda.org.uk/

Invest Northern Ireland: http://www.investni.com/index.asp

London Development Agency: http://www.lda.gov.uk/

North West Development Agency: http://www.nwda.co.uk

One NorthEast: http://www.onenortheast.co.uk

Scottish Enterprise: http://www.scottish-enterprise.com

South East England Development Agency (SEEDA): http://www.seeda.co.uk/

South West of England Development Agency: http://www. southwestengland.co.uk/

Welsh Assembly Government: http://www.wales.gov.uk

Yorkshire Forward: http://www.yorkshire-forward.com

For more information on the business support service offered by the DTI please visit: www.dti.gov.uk/innovation/index.

For a wider source of practical advice and support for small businesses please visit: www.Businesslink.gov.uk.

7.6 The Design Council

The Design Council is working to strengthen the UK's economy by helping businesses understand the value of design and use it to make themselves more competitive.

It has created a national business support programme offering companies direct support through a range of services that provide hands-on help to companies from start-ups to established businesses.

The Designing Demand programme is due to launch in two regions in October 2006, and is scheduled to be available nationally by 2008. It is a direct result of the Cox Review of Creativity in Business, undertaken by Design Council Chairman Sir George Cox and commissioned by Chancellor of the Exchequer Gordon Brown. The review underlined the competitive threat posed to the UK by fast emerging global economies. It argued that, with their overseas rivals moving beyond low-cost manufacturing and into high-value goods, UK businesses will only be able to survive by developing new offerings driven by creativity.

Design is a key process for generating business ideas and shaping them into competitive products and services, but many businesses still use it late in the development cycle, where its role is restricted to styling.

In contrast, businesses which use design to lead strategy and product and service development get measurable results. Design Council research shows that for every £100 design-led businesses invest in design, they get an average of £225 back in increased sales. Similarly, businesses which use design see benefits across practically every measure of performance, including market share, growth, share price, productivity and competitiveness.

The Cox Review made the case for using design at a strategic level in business and one of its key recommendations, approved by the Chancellor, was to provide support for businesses to help them get maximum value from design.

The Designing Demand programme is the result. It has been extensively, and successfully, piloted and is now being delivered through Regional Development Agencies.

The programme includes:

- **Designing Demand Workshops** – one-day sessions using a mixture of case studies and live exercises to demonstrate how design can be used to make business decisions, not just implement them. The workshops are led by experienced design managers who also help participants investigate how design could drive better performance in their own companies.

After the workshop, there are three more services offering direct support tailored to different needs, from a single design project to an intensive 18-month examination of business strategy:

- **Accelerate** helps businesses devise and run a single design project over five to 12 months. It provides up to five days' support from a Design Associate experienced in managing design and dealing with business issues. Businesses using the service benefit directly from their design project, but their management teams also develop skills they can use in the future to crack strategic issues.

- **Innovate** is aimed at businesses commercializing new technology. It provides up to 18 months of support to help companies use design to attract investment, develop strategy and boost market presence. The service gives an introduction to how design can get technology to market faster and reduce risk. Then participants explore potential design opportunities and projects in their own businesses with Design Associates. One project is then implemented over the next year.

- **Immerse** is the most intensive of the services, aimed at established businesses. Management teams work with leading designers to examine their business in detail. The design team highlights a range of opportunities for design to overcome a key business challenge and make a lasting impact. The business then decides which of the opportunities to follow up and implements them over 18 months, with backing from a Design Associate. Alongside new skills including choosing, briefing and managing designers, managers develop a new way of thinking about how to take their business forward.

Designing Demand has been tested with businesses across the UK. All the companies taking part saw substantial benefits. Among manufacturers, for instance, turnover rose by 14 per cent above predicted levels and 88 per cent of businesses rated their design projects as critical to success.

The Design Council also supports businesses with knowledge and information about design, mostly provided online. The Value of Design Factfinder, a unique online information tool, features research demonstrating the link between the use of design and better business performance.

In particular, it shows that:

- Two-thirds of companies who ignore design have to compete mainly on price. In companies where design is integral, just one-third do so.
- More than eight out of ten design-led companies have introduced a new product or service in the last three years, compared to just 40 per cent of UK companies overall.
- Design is integral to 39 per cent of rapidly growing companies but to only 7 per cent of static ones.
- 80 per cent of design-led businesses have opened up new markets in the last three years. Only 42 per cent of UK businesses overall have done so.
- A business that increases its investment in design is more than twice as likely to see its turnover grow as a business that does not do so.

For more information on all the Design Council's work, visit: www.designcouncil.org.uk.

For more information on Designing Demand, visit: www.designingdemand.org.uk.

taking it further

The following list contains some contact details you may find useful. It is not a full list but it does provide a good starting point.

Patent Office Central Enquiry Unit
Website: www.patent.gov.uk
Phone: 0845 9500505

The British Library
Website: www.bl.uk/business
Phone: 0207 412 7903

The European Patent Office
Website: www.european-patent-office.org
Phone: +0049 89 2399 4636

Office for Harmonization in the Internal Market
Website: www.oami.europa.eu.
Phone: +0034 96 513 9100

The Chartered Institute of Patent Attorneys
Website: www.cipa.org.uk
Phone: 0207 405 9450

The Institute of Trade Mark Attorneys
Website: www.itma.org.uk
Phone: 0208 686 2052

Alliance Against Counterfeiting and Piracy
Website: www.aacp.org.uk
Phone: 0207 534 0595

British Phonographic Industry (BPI)
Website: www.bpi.co.uk
Phone: 0207 803 1300

Federation Against Copyright Theft
Website: www.fact-uk.org.uk
Phone: 0208 568 6646

Business Link (England)
Website: www.businesslink.gov.uk
Phone: 0845 600 9006

Invest Northern Ireland
Website:www.investni.com
Phone: 0289 023 9090

Innovators Counselling and Advisory Services for Scotland
(ICASS)
Website: www.icass.co.uk
Phone: 0141 572 8395

Intellectual Asset Centre (Scotland)
Website: www.ia-centre.org.uk
Phone: 0141 243 4920,

Business Gateway (Scotland)
Website: www.bgateway.com
Phone: 0845 609 6611

Business Eye (Wales)
Website: www.businesseye.org.uk
Phone: 0845 796 9798

Ideas 21
Website: www.ideas21.co.uk
Phone: 0208 780 9017

The British Chambers of Commerce
Website: www.chamberonline.co.uk
Phone: 0207 654 5800

Trading Standards Institute
Website: www.tsi.org.uk
Phone: 0870 872 9000

UK Trade and Investment
Website: www.uktradeinvest.gov.uk
Phone: 0207 215 8000

Anti-copying in Design
Website: www.acid.uk.com
Phone: 0845 644 3617

HM Revenue and Customs
Website: www.hmrc.gov.uk
Phone: 0845 010 9000

The Department of Trade and Industry
Website: www.dti.gov.uk
Phone: 020 7215 5000

index

advertising
  designs registration **91**
  trade marks in **14–15**
African Intellectual Property
        Organization (OAPI) **130**
African Regional Intellectual
        Property Organization
        (APIPO) **130**
after-the-event insurance (ATE)
        102–3
attorneys
  patent **84**
  trade mark **86, 87, 88, 89**
audits *see* intellectual property audit
AURIL (Association of University
        Research Industry Links) **74–5**
authorship, and copyright **96–7**

before-the-event insurance **100–2**
Berne Convention for the Protection
        of Literary and Artistic Works
        148
biotechnology **11**
brand names **8**
  preventing counterfeiting and
        piracy **110–11**
British Technology Group (BTG) **36,
        37**
business adviser networks **30–3**
business–university collaboration
        70–7
businesses
  and the European Community
        Trade Mark (CTM) **132–3**
  importance of intellectual
        property to **8–9**
  making money from intellectual
        property **33–8**
  see also company names; SMEs
        (small and medium-sized
        enterprises)

China **1, 5, 58**
CIPA (Chartered Institute of Patent
        Agents) **160**
collaborative research and
        development, DTI funding
        for **166**
commissioned works, and
        copyright **97–8**
Community Patent Convention
        (CPC) **122–4**
Community Trade Mark *see*
        European Community Trade
        Mark (CTM)
company names **111–17**
  conflict with an existing business
        name **113**
  conflict with a registered trade
        mark **113–14**
  domain names **17, 26–7, 116–17**
  name 'too like' name of an
        existing company **112**
  registering company name as a
        trade mark **114–16**
  setting up the company and
        choice of name **111–12**
computer programs, patenting **11**

conditional fee arrangements **103–4**
confidentiality, and licensing **60, 65**
Confidentiality Agreements (CDAs) **61**
contact lenses, invention of daily
        disposable **33–8**
copyright **2–3, 8, 9, 23–5**
    activities covered by **23**
    as an unregistered right **23–4**
    audits **42, 45, 47**
    claiming and enforcing **94–6**
    duration of UK copyright **24–5**
    exceptions to **25**
    and ideas **24**
    insurance **104**
    international protection **148**
    length of rights period **3**
    limited use of copyright works **25**
    looking after **94–8**
    ownership **41–2, 96–8**
        commissioned works **97–8**
        more than one person **96–7**
        transferring **97**
    types of work protected **24**
counterfeiting **104–5**
    advice for brand owners **110–11**
    criminal offences **106–7**
    disclaimers **109**
    enforcement agencies **108–9**
    legal position of traders **109, 110**
    relevant legal provisions relating
        to **105–6**
courts
    Community trade mark **136–7**
    and infringement of IP rights **92**
    plans to establish a European
        Patent Court **124**
Cox Review of Creativity in
        Business **169**
CPC (Community Patent
        Convention) **122–4**
Cranfield University, and the
        Lambert Model Agreements
        Toolkit **74**
crime prevention *see* enforcement
        of IP rights
CTM *see* European Community
        Trade Mark (CTM)
cybersquatters, and domain name
        disputes **28**

database searching **49–58**
    designs registration **49, 57–8**
    patents **49–55**
    registered trade marks **49, 55–7**
Department of Trade and Industry
        (DTI), business support
        services **165–9**
design audits **43, 44**
Design Council **169–71**
designs registration **8, 9, 19–23**
    database searching **49, 57–8**
        Locarno classification
            scheme **57–8**
    design right **20, 90–1**
    European Community designs **20,
        21, 22, 143–8**
        advantages of registration **146**
        defining a 'design' **144–5**
        e-filing applications **148**
        and the Hague Agreement **147**
        and individual character **145**
        'new' designs **145**
        protection **146–7**
        registered **143–4**
        unregistered **144**
    insurance **100**
    legal protection of **107**
    licensing **20, 93**
    looking after
        advertising **91**
        court proceedings **92**
        enforcement agencies **91**
        mediation **92**
        notification **91**
        primary and secondary
            infringement **94**
        unregistered design rights **93**
    looking after designs **90–4**
    products covered by **19**
    in the UK **21**
    useful tips for designers **22–3**
digitization, and IP enforcement **4**
disclaimers, for counterfeit goods
        109
domain name system (DNS) **17,
        26–7**
    checking if a name is available
        26–7
    disputes **28**

registers **26**
renewing domain names **27**
and trade marks **28**
DTI *see* Department of Trade and
    Industry (DTI)

ECLA patent classification scheme
    52–3
EMI **2**
employers, and copyright ownership
    96
enforcement of IP rights **4–5, 104–11**
copyright **95–6**
counterfeiting and piracy **104–5**
designs registration **91**
enforcement agencies **91, 108–9**
relevant legislation **105–7**
EPC (European Patent Convention)
    9, 119, 122–3
EPLA (European Patent Litigation
    Agreement) **124**
EPO *see* European Patent Office
    (EPO)
Esher, Lord **98**
esp@cenet database **50–1, 53, 55**
Eurasian Patent Organization (OAPI)
    130
European Commission design
    regulations **143**
European Community
Community designs **20, 21, 22,
    143–8**
imports of counterfeited and
    pirated goods **109**
and the Madrid System **139**
European Community Trade Mark
    (CTM) **17, 132–7**
applications for **133–4**
absolute grounds for refusal
    134
opposition **134–5**
registration **135**
characteristics **133**
as a company asset **132, 132–3**
courts **136–7**
database **55**
and national trade mark
    registration systems **135–6**
statistics on **137**

European Patent Convention (EPC)
    9, 119, 122–3
European Patent Litigation
    Agreement (EPLA) **124**
European Patent Office (EPO) **10,
    13, 119–25, 130**
applications **119–21**
classification scheme (ECLA) **52–3**
Community patent **122–4**
esp@cenet database **50–1, 53, 55**
London Agreement **125**
official languages **119, 121**
On-Line File Inspection **53–4**
'Opposition' procedure **85, 121–2**
regional protection of patents **83**
Rule 34 period **121**
external intellectual property audit
    40

'family matching', and patent
    databases **53**
films, and copyright **24, 96, 97**
FireAngel® story **77–80**
flexibility of IP **2, 3, 5**
'freedom to operate' searches, of
    patent databases **54**

Government role in IP **2, 6**

Hague Agreement **147**
Hertfordshire University, and the
    Lambert Model Agreements
    Toolkit **74**
HM Revenue and Customs (HMRC),
    and enforcement of IP rights
    91, 109

IBM **3**
ideas, and copyright **24**
Index of Company Names **111, 112**
Industrial Property (IP) Offices, in
    European countries **136**
infringement proceedings
and copyright **95–6**
and design rights
court proceedings **92**
groundless threats of **92–3**
licensing **92**
mediation **92**

primary and secondary
infringement **94**
unregistered **93**
and design threat **91–3**
and intellectual property
insurance **100–2, 104**
registered trade marks **114**
infringement searches, of patent
databases **54**
innovation, and NESTA **150–3**
insurance of intellectual property ·
98–104
after the event **102–3**
before the event **100–2**
and litigation costs **98–9, 102–3**
conditional fee arrangements
103–4
professional indemnity insurance
100
Intellectual Assets (IA) Centre **30–3**
intellectual property audits **40–8**
copyright audits **42, 45, 47**
copyright ownership **41–2**
design audits **43, 44**
examples in practice **43–8**
external **40**
internal **40**
ownership of intellectual property
41–2
patent audits **42, 43–4, 45–6, 47–8**
patented technology **41**
product names **41**
trade marks **42, 44, 46, 48**
working out an IP strategy **43**
intellectual property rights **7–28**
copyright **2–3, 8, 9, 23–5**
designs registration **8, 9, 19–23**
importance to business **8–9**
patents **3–4, 8, 9, 10–14**
trade marks **8–9, 14–19**
internal intellectual property audit **40**
International copyright protection
148
International Patent Classification
scheme (IPC) **51–2, 53**
international patent protection
125–31
filing an international application
128

national phase of application
129–30
Patent Cooperation Treaty (PCT)
**9, 13, 14, 83, 125, 127–8,
130, 131**
publication of applications **129**
search report **129**
International Searching Authorities
(ISAs) **129**
international trade mark registration
17, 136, 137–42
Madrid System **17, 55, 137, 138–9,
140–1, 142**
managing **142**
reasons for **137–8**
Internet **3**
domain names **17, 26–7, 116–17**
enforcing copyright for work on
websites **95**
and European Community
designs, e-filing applications
148
inventor club websites **156**
trade mark registers **18**
invention promoters **157–60**
inventor clubs **154–7**
inventors, and licensing **59, 60**
IP (intellectual property) debate **1–2**
ISAs (International Searching
Authorities) **129**

Japanese Patent Office **50**

knowledge transfer networks **165**
knowledge transfer partnerships **167**
knowledge-based economy **1, 4, 40**

Lambert Model Agreement Toolkit
70–7
Agreement Outline **72, 76**
Decision Guide **72, 75, 76**
elements **71–2**
feedback and uptake **74–6**
Guidance Notes **71, 72**
material transfer agreement (MTA)
73
non-disclosure agreement (NDA)
73
origin **71**

purpose **70–1**
licensing intellectual property **58–68,
   79**
   access **65**
   common mistakes **59–60**
   defining a licence **58–9**
   due diligence exercise **60–5**
      aims **62**
      competition **63**
      IP and patent **63–4**
      IP valuation **64**
      manufacturing **64**
      markets **63**
      reasons for carrying out **60–2**
      scientific **64**
      time factors **64–5**
      understanding risk and rewards
         62
   maintaining IP value **67**
   negotiation **66**
   paperwork **65**
   patents **9, 14, 58–68, 85**
   physical transfer **65**
   registered designs **20, 93**
   show-how and know-how **65**
litigation costs, and insurance **98–9,
   102–3, 104**
Locarno classification scheme, for
   registered designs **57–8**
London Agreement (2000) **125**
looking after intellectual property
   81–117
   copyright **94–8**
   designs **90–4**
   patents **82–5**
   trade marks **86–90**

Madrid System for the International
   Registration of Marks **17, 55,
   137, 138–9, 140–1, 142**
Manufacturing Advisory Service
   (MAS) **161–5**
manufacturing industry, example of
   IP audit in practice **47–8**
Marx, Groucho **157**
MAS (Manufacturing Advisory
   Service) **161–5**
Material Transfer Agreements
   (MTAs) **61**

mediation
   and infringement of IP rights **92**
   and SMEs **99**
micro projects, DTI grants for **167**
Microsoft IP Venture Licensing
   Programme **3**
mining patents **82**
money-making from intellectual
   property **33–8, 77–80**
MP3 players **5**

names of companies *see* company
   names
National Endowment for Science,
   Technology and the Arts
   (NESTA) **150–3**
national trade mark registration
   systems **135–6**
negotiation
   licensing intellectual property **66**
   using the Lambert Model
      Agreements Toolkit **70–7**
NESTA (National Endowment for
   Science, Technology and the
   Arts) **150–3**
Nice classification of trade marks **56**
Nominet **27**
Non Disclosure Agreements (NDAs)
   61
Northern Ireland **108**
'novelty' searches, of patent
   databases **54**

OHIM (Office of Harmonization for
   the Internal Market)
   and design registration **143–4,
      146, 147**
   and trade marks **55, 132, 133–6,
      143**
Option Agreements **61, 64**
ownership of intellectual property
   41–2
Oxford University, and the Lambert
   Model Agreements Toolkit **74**

Paris Convention on the Protection
   of Industrial Property **126**
patent attorneys **84**

Patent Cooperation Treaty (PCT) **9,
    13, 14, 83, 125, 127–8, 130,
    131**
Patent Office **4, 5, 9**
    and design registration **21, 91**
    and domain name registrations **27**
    and international applications **128**
    and invention promoters **159**
    and the Manufacturing Advisory
        Service (MAS) **161, 162**
    obtaining a patent **13**
    and trade mark registration **89, 114**
    Trade Marks Search and Advisory
        Service **114, 115–16**
    see also European Patent Office
        (EPO)
Patent Status Information Service
    (UK) **53**
patents **3–4, 8, 9, 10–14**
    audits **42, 43–4, 45–6, 47–8**
    claims **11, 12**
    computer programs **11**
    database searching **49–55**
        classification schemes **51–3**
        'family matching' **53**
        'freedom to operate' searches
            54
        infringement searches **54**
        legal status of **53–4**
        'novelty' searches **54**
        PATLIB centres **54–5**
        reasons to search **54**
        'state-of-the-art' searches **54**
        'value-added' search services **55**
    descriptions **11–12**
    determining patentable inventions
        10
    insurance **100, 104**
    licensing **9, 14, 58–68, 85**
    looking after **82–5**
        annual renewal fees **84**
        choosing a patenting strategy
            82–4
        enforcing patents **84–5**
        getting a patent granted **84**
        infringements **83**
        international patent application
            system **83**
        mining **82**

    obtaining **12–14**
    raising funding for early-stage
        companies **14**
    renewal fees **14**
    right to sue an infringer **14**
    Supplementary Protection
        Certificates **14**
    see also European Patent
        Convention (EPC); Patent
        Office
PATLIB centres **54–4**
PCT see Patent Cooperation Treaty
    (PCT)
pharmaceutical industry **11, 14**
piracy **104–5**
    advice for brand owners **110–11**
    criminal offences **106–7**
    enforcement agencies **108–9**
police, and enforcement of IP rights
    108

RDAs (Regional Development
    Agencies) **75, 161, 168**
regional patent systems **130**
Registered Designs Regulations
    2001 **20**
registered trade marks (RTMs) **41**
research and development, DTI
    funding for **166, 167–8**
rights see intellectual property rights
Rutter, Nick **77–9**

Scotland, Intellectual Assets (IA)
    Centre **30–3**
Seden, Bill **33, 34, 35**
service industry, example of IP audit
    in practice **43–5**
SMEs (small and medium-sized
    enterprises)
    choosing a patent strategy **84**
    and intellectual property
        insurance **98–104**
    international protection
        patents **125–31**
        trade marks **139**
    licensing intellectual property
        58–68
    and the Manufacturing Advisory
        Service (MAS) **161**

see also company names
software industry, example of IP
audit in practice **45–7**
sound recordings
and copyright **24, 96**
legal protection against piracy
107
Sprue Aegis **78, 80**

Tate, Sam **77–9**
TellPat **4–5**
third-party intellectual property **40**
establishing ownership **48**
patents **54, 85**
trade mark attorneys **86, 87, 88, 89**
Trade Mark Offices **16–17**
trade marks **8–9, 14–19**
and advertising **14–15**
assignment and licensing **18, 19**
audits **42, 44, 46, 48**
clearance **18**
and company names **113–16**
database searching **49, 55–7**
Nice classification **56**
reasons for searching **56–7**
distinctiveness of **15–16**
and domain names **28**
insurance **104**
and intellectual property audits **41**
looking after **86–90**
correct use of **87**
descriptive words and phrases
in **88**
legal requirements **87**
lost rights **88**
marking symbols **88**
reviewing trade mark portfolios
86
tips **90**
non-use **18**
professional help **19**
protection **16–17**
European protection system
132–7
legal protection for
counterfeiting/unauthorized
use of **105**
registered trade marks (RTMs) **41,
114**

registration **16, 17**
change in UK law **89–90**
international **17, 136, 137–42**
limitations of **18**
renewal fees **87**
value **19**
watching services **57, 89–90**
Trade-Related Aspects of
Intellectual Property Rights
(TRIPs Agreement) **109, 148**
traders, and counterfeit goods **109,
110**
Trading Standards Officers, and
enforcement of IP rights
108–9
TRIPs Agreement **109, 148**

UCC (Universal Copyright
Convention) **148**
UK legislation
Business Names Act (1985) **113**
Companies Act (1985) **113**
Copyright, Designs and Patents
Act (1988) **105–6, 107**
Copyright, etc. and Trade Marks
(Offences and Enforcement)
Act (2002) **106**
Registered Designs Act (1949) **19,
90–1, 92–3**
Trade Descriptions Act (1968) **105**
Trade Marks Act (1938) **109**
Trade Marks Act (1994) **105, 106,
110**
United States Patent and Trademark
Office **40**
Universal Copyright Convention
(UCC) **148**
universities **69–80**
collaborative research and
development **70–7**
making money from IP **77–80**
university-derived IP and
licensing **59**

World Intellectual Property
Organization (WIPO) **28, 50,
55, 128, 129, 139, 141**

setting up a small business
vera hughes and david weller

- Are you setting up a small business?
- Do you need help to define what you have to offer?
- Are you looking for guidance in marketing and finance?

Setting up a Small Business, now in its fourth edition, gives you clear, concise information and guidance in all aspects of setting up a small business, including legal requirements, IT, finance and staffing issues.

Vera Hughes and **David Weller** started their own business in 1980 and have a wide experience of many areas of commerce. In addition to the phenomenally successful **Setting up a Small Business** they have written a number of books on retailing.